To: Laura Alison
Snyder
12/25/98'

Since I will be living in
Santa Barbara for a few years now
that I am attending UCSB, I thought
You too would like to know a little bit
more about the area.

Love you always,
Your daughter,
Laura Leigh
Holmstrom

D1064780

Santa Barbara

Published by Longstreet Press, Inc.
A subsidiary of Cox Newspapers
A subsidiary of Cox Enterprises, Inc.
2140 Newmarket Parkway, Suite 118
Marietta, Georgia 30067

Text © 1996 by Marcia Meier
Photography © 1996 by James Chen

All rights reserved. No part of this book may be reproduced in any form by
any means without the prior written permission of the Publisher, excepting brief
quotations used in connection with reviews, written specifically for inclusion
in a magazine or newspaper.

Printed in the United States of America

1st printing, 1996

Library of Congress No. 96-76739

ISBN: 1-56352-293-4

This book was printed by Quebecor/Kingsport, Tennessee.

Digital film prep and separations by Advertising Technologies, Inc., Atlanta, Georgia

MANAGING EDITOR
Erica Fox

ART DIRECTION AND PRODUCTION
Graham & Company Graphics, Inc.
Marietta, Georgia

Santa Barbara

PARADISE ON THE PACIFIC

TEXT BY
MARCIA MEIER

PHOTOGRAPHY BY
JAMES CHEN

LONGSTREET PRESS
Atlanta, Georgia

PUBLISHED IN COOPERATION WITH THE
SANTA BARBARA CHAMBER OF COMMERCE

CONTENTS

FOREWORD

Santa Barbara is a special community. More than a place, it represents a standard of excellence. The natural beauty of our surroundings and the gracious blend of old and new in our Mediterranean-style architecture are known around the world.

We are blessed with an extraordinary quality of life. The low-rise buildings of downtown provide the intimacy of a small town, yet our cultural and artistic offerings are comparable to those in a bigger city. We have an excellent symphony, a chamber orchestra, a light opera company, and outstanding choral groups. There are three first-rate hospitals in the greater Santa Barbara area, as well as fine schools, including the renowned University of California at Santa Barbara.

Santa Barbara is an old city, dating from 1782. It was established as a Spanish military presidio and mission near a cluster of Chumash Indian villages. Recognition of our Spanish colonial heritage is reflected in the presentation and restoration of our historic buildings.

The quaint architecture of these buildings and their pedestrian environment are carefully maintained as new buildings are added to meet contemporary needs. It is this gracious blend of old and new that gives Santa Barbara the special flavor treasured by residents and admired by visitors.

Santa Barbara offers the benefits of a small town with the business climate of an international city. A growing segment of our business community is made up of companies that develop critical medical apparatus and innovative testing equipment. The 1990s have brought an increase in telecommunications and software development. These ventures are ideal for balancing economic growth and our community goals.

Paseo Nuevo shopping center, an outdoor mall whose design reflects the series of pedestrian "paseos" that wind through the downtown, is the newest addition to our thriving retail district. Along State Street and out onto Stearns Wharf, year-round indoor and outdoor dining opportunities contribute to a tourist trade par excellence.

Offering a relaxed atmosphere in a beautiful environment just two hours north of Los Angeles, Santa Barbara presents a refreshing change from large metropolitan areas. Yet with its modern airport and freeway and rail connections, it remains accessible.

We are proud of our quality of life and strong sense of community, our traditions, and our gracious hospitality. We welcome you to Santa Barbara and invite you to discover the paradise we call home.

MAYOR HARRIET MILLER
CITY OF SANTA BARBARA

INTRODUCTION

SANTA BARBARA IS ONE OF THE MOST BEAUTIFUL PLACES IN THE WORLD. NESTLED BETWEEN THE SANTA YNEZ MOUNTAINS ON THE NORTH AND THE PACIFIC OCEAN ON THE SOUTH, THE GREATER CITY AREA STRETCHES OUT ON A STRIP OF COASTLINE ONLY 4 MILES WIDE AND 12 MILES LONG.

*d*ecked in red-tile roofs and appointed with towering palm trees, the city reaches from the foothills toward the glistening sea. Golden-sand beaches and coastal cliffs beckon sun worshipers and recreationists alike.

The natural beauty of the surroundings combined with a moderate Mediterranean climate give Santa Barbara a resort atmosphere. The average year-round temperature is 70 degrees, the average rainfall about 18 inches. Temperate fog on summer mornings, burning off most days before noon, keeps things cool. In the spring and fall, warm, sunny days make living and working in Santa Barbara seem like a perpetual vacation.

But Santa Barbara's natural beauty is only part of its identity. Its Spanish-Mexican heritage is evident nearly everywhere—in the city's graceful architectural style, featuring white stucco and red-tile roofs, in the historic Spanish presidio and yearly four-day Fiesta celebration, and in the commitment to community its people exhibit every single day.

The greater region—called the South Coast—has been rated among the top 10 safest urban areas in the West by the FBI. Air quality is the best in Southern California. Traffic congestion is minimal.

Education is of high quality and a strong influence throughout the community, from elementary-school level through graduate study. The University of California's small but prestigious Santa Barbara campus (UCSB) graces a point on the ocean and features disciplines of study that reflect the community: theoretical studies, marine sciences, environmental studies, physics, business. It has been ranked one of the world's finest research universities, offering a brain trust and high-tech atmosphere conducive to the development of knowledge-based industries.

The community also boasts several private educational institutions, including Westmont College, a noted Christian school. One of the best community colleges in California—Santa Barbara City College—is here as well.

For a city its size, Santa Barbara is unequaled in the cultural arts. There are dozens of performing and visual arts organizations, and the three colleges provide additional arts offerings of exceptional quality. The venerable Santa Barbara Symphony delights audiences season after season, and the private Music Academy of the West's summer sessions attract top music students from around the world.

Businesses are here because they want to be a part of the natural environment and the community. Many—like the Territory Ahead and Jandd—started out as small cottage industries and grew into major players in the world of commerce. Others, like the national health care giant Tenet Healthcare Corporation, have moved to the area recently. Tenet moved its corporate headquarters and 90 top executives from Santa Monica to Santa Barbara in early 1996.

Thirty minutes to the north of Santa Barbara is the lovely and bucolic Santa Ynez Valley, where the vineyards and wineries produce some of the finest wines in the world and the owners of the vast ranches raise race horses and ostriches.

The vibrant Los Angeles basin is only 100 miles to the south. Just a few hours away by car are Los Angeles International Airport, Six Flags Magic Mountain, Disneyland, Universal Studios, Hollywood, first-rate theater, wintertime skiing in the mountains above L.A., and many other offerings.

A few hours farther up the coast is San Francisco—the romantic City by the Bay—featuring the stunning Golden Gate Bridge, Union Square, Fisherman's Wharf, shopping, and theater. From San Francisco, Stanford University and Silicon Valley are just a short drive south.

There are lots of wonderful places just north and south of Santa Barbara, but, as people who live here quickly discover, there's little need to go anywhere when home is Paradise on the Pacific.

The Nordstrom tower (left) reflects the Moorish influence on Santa Barbara's architecture. Above, a colorful carpet of lupine on Figueroa Mountain, above Santa Barbara.

The Mission Rose Garden,
across from the Santa Barbara
Mission, is tenderly cared for
by a group of volunteers.

THE DOLPHIN FOUNTAIN, at the foot of Stearns Wharf, sculpted by Santa Barbara artist Bud Bottoms, has become an important symbol for the city.

THE HISTORIC SANTA BARBARA
County Courthouse (left),
designed by William Mooser
and Co. and built in 1927–29,
is considered one of the most
important public monuments
of the Spanish colonial revival
in the United States. Above,
agapanthus bloom in the side
garden of one of Santa Barbara's
beautiful churches.

ONE

SANTA BARBARA IN HISTORICAL PERSPECTIVE

SANTA BARBARA'S PAST IS AS ROMAN-
TIC AS THE CITY IS TODAY. SPANISH
CONQUISTADORS, MEXICAN DONS,
MISSION PADRES, AND THE CREATION OVER
TIME OF AN ENTRANCING AND BEAUTIFUL
ARCHITECTURAL STYLE INFORMED AND INFLU-
ENCED THE CITY AND ITS CITIZENS. THE
MEDITERRANEAN-LIKE CLIMATE AND COASTAL
LOCATION ARE AND WERE ENTICING. FROM
WHAT WE KNOW ABOUT THE SOUTH COAST'S
FIRST INHABITANTS, THEY THOUGHT THEY
HAD DISCOVERED PARADISE.

FIRST SETTLERS

The first settlers of the region were a gentle people called the Chumash. They lived along the Pacific Ocean from Malibu on the south to San Luis Obispo on the north and offshore on the Channel Islands.

The Chumash lived on an abundance of shellfish and other seafood, small wild game, berries, and other vegetation. They are credited with being the architects of the first plank canoe, called a *tomol*, and with having complex religious and community customs. They were particularly adept at craftsmanship and noted for their basketry.

When the Spanish explorer Juan Rodriguez Cabrillo sailed up the coast of California in 1542, he discovered numerous Chumash villages. Anthropologists and archaeologists have placed the age of some Chumash artifacts found in the Santa Barbara area at about 1,000 years old. Early hunting peoples are believed to have inhabited the area 9,000 years ago.

Cabrillo's was the first documented contact with the Chumash, and until the mid-1700s, there were only three others—in 1587, 1595, and 1602.

Santa Barbara got its name during an expedition by Sebastian Vizcaino in 1602. Vizcaino's ship sailed into the channel between the mainland and the islands after a violent storm. A thankful monk on board the ship, noting that it was the eve of the feast day of Saint Barbara, December 3, bestowed her name upon the channel.

CREATION OF THE CITY

In 1769, the explorer Gaspar de Portola, at the behest of the king of Spain, led an expedition from Mexico to establish presidios, or forts, and missions in Alta California. The striking Santa Barbara Mission and the city's presidio, now under restoration, were part of this effort, which eventually led to the founding of 21 missions between San Diego and Sonoma, north of San Francisco.

The founding of the Santa Barbara Mission and the Spanish presidio, in April 1782, jointly signaled the creation of the city that would become modern-day Santa Barbara. The governor of California, Felipe de Neve, had received directions in 1775 from the king of Spain to establish Monterey as the seat of Alta California's government. Because none of the missions between San Diego and Monterey had the protection of a presidio, Neve decided to found one along the coastline near the Channel Islands.

Neve and Father Junípero Serra, the father of most of California's missions, were accompanied by Captain José Francisco Ortega on that April trip. Ortega ultimately became *comandante* of the newly established Santa Barbara Presidio, founded at the corner of what are now Santa Barbara and Canon Perdido Streets.

MISSION PERIOD

The period that followed, during which the mission padres attempted to convert the Native Americans to Christianity, led to the destruction of the Chumash culture and way of life and very nearly wiped out the tribe. Diseases brought from Europe decimated the villages over time, and the religious and social customs of the Chumash went by the wayside as they embraced Catholicism.

Mission Santa Barbara—often called the "Queen of the Missions" because of its profound beauty—was begun in 1786 and dedicated in 1820, eight years after a large earthquake shook the original mission structure to the ground. It was rebuilt, this time under the influence of an ancient Roman architectural compiler named Vitruvius. His work informs many of the attempts at mission restoration that swept California in the 1820s and 1830s. Mission Santa Barbara looks today essentially as it did at the 1820 dedication.

The founding of the presidio began a long period of Spanish-Mexican rule in which military and church were tightly intertwined. Spanish land grants led to the creation of large ranchos within the Santa Barbara district, and it became one of the wealthiest of the districts under the governor at Monterey. This colonial period of Santa Barbara's history lent the city its distinct and beautiful architectural style—white stucco buildings and red-tile roofs.

In 1821, Mexico declared its independence from Spain, and Alta California became a territory of Mexico. The presidio continued to govern the city and remained an important aspect of Santa Barbara life and culture until 1846, when General John C. Fremont and his American

battalion came over the San Marcos Pass in the mountains north of the city and raised the U.S. flag at Santa Barbara. In 1848, California officially became a U.S. territory. On April 9, 1850, Santa Barbara became a legal city. Later that year, California became the 31st state in the Union.

With the secularization of the missions in 1834 came the gradual loss of the mission system at Santa Barbara. The holdings and land were leased, the Chumash inhabitants of mission housing ultimately left, and the church was turned over to the Franciscans, who remain at the mission today.

EMERGENCE AS A "MORE BEAUTIFUL PLACE"

On June 29, 1925, the Queen of the Missions was heavily damaged by earthquake again, but the community regrouped and rebuilt. Beginning in May 1926, the entire church was restored with as much of the original building materials as possible. The church was completed in 1927 and celebrated with the opening of the newly established Old Spanish Days Fiesta on August 10.

The 1925 earthquake also opened the door for the reconstruction of the city using its now-signature Spanish colonial architectural style. The temblor toppled buildings all over town. While cradled in a natural setting striking for its beauty, the town was a hodgepodge of architectural styles. Adobe dwellings from presidio days existed in various states of repair all around the community. In the 1850s, the Americans introduced Victorian-style brick, and, later, frame houses, and laid out the city on a grid system.

By the early 1900s, the city had a chaotic feel to it. Pearl Chase, who was to become one of the city's most influential pioneers in creating its ultimate style and image, related her impression of the town upon returning from studies at the University of California at Berkeley in 1907: "I remember alighting from the train at the old Victoria Street station, coming home for the holidays, and how ashamed I was of Santa Barbara's shabby buildings, dusty streets and lack of landscaping. Then and there I resolved to dedicate myself to making Santa Barbara a more beautiful place to live in."

That is exactly what she did. In 1920, Chase and other prominent Santa Barbarans established the Community Arts Association to promote the beautification of the city by preserving old adobes and encouraging new construction in the Spanish style.

At left, adobe brick is formed and sun-baked for the reconstruction of the old presidio. Above, a model, in the forefront, offers a view of how the fort will look after it has been rebuilt.

One of the most illustrative buildings of the period—the El Paseo, which included the historic de la Guerra family adobe—was one of the few structures to withstand the 1925 tremor. Its endurance convinced the community that the Spanish colonial style of architecture was not only in keeping with the environment but structurally sound.

After the quake, the Community Arts Association's Plans and Planting Committee prevailed upon the city council to establish an architectural review board and new guidelines to ensure that the rebuilt city would reflect the dedicated look.

Red-tile roofs, graceful arches, stucco walls, and wrought-iron ornamentation became *de rigueur* in design. Today, the sight of the city from the foothills is breathtaking for its red-and-white sea of structures against the blue of the Pacific.

PLAYGROUND TO THE RICH AND FAMOUS

In the early 1900s, Santa Barbara and Montecito became favorite haunts of the rich and famous. The climate, natural beauty, and mineral springs attracted those who sought refuge from a bustling world. The community remains an escape for the wealthy from Los Angeles and the East Coast. Montecito particularly is the site of vast, breathtaking estates hidden behind tall hedges and walls.

Between 1912 and 1921, Santa Barbara also became home to the largest movie studio. Flying A Studios was built at the northwest corner of State and Mission Streets, and for a time it made the city the film capital of the world. The studio—and the movie stars who came with it—added to the city's allure.

Many of the wealthy people who moved here—either to retire or spend time at second (or third) homes—became guiding forces behind the movement to preserve and beautify the city.

Among these people were Dwight Murphy, a multi-millionaire who made his money in railroads and retired—at the age of 41—to Santa Barbara in 1925. Max Fleischmann, the yeast king, lived in Summerland, a small community on the South Coast, from 1921 to 1956. William H. Bliss, a wealthy St. Louis attorney, came to Montecito before World War I. He and his New York socialite wife built

PEARL CHASE

Pearl Chase was a monumental force in the beautification of Santa Barbara. Her efforts from the early 1920s through the 1970s aimed at preserving the city's graceful Spanish colonial style of architecture are in large part responsible for the city's profound attractiveness.

Pearl was the daughter of Hezekiah "Hezzie" Griggs Chase and Maria "Nina" Dempsey Chase. Her grandfather, also Hezekiah, owned a profitable shoe factory in Boston. When the elder Chase went blind, Hezzie left college to run the business. But while Pearl and her brother, Harold, were still quite young, Hezzie was severely injured by a falling steel warehouse door.

Hezzie Chase recovered, but it was a slow process. Pearl's mother had heard that the climate and mineral springs in Santa Barbara were restorative and convinced Hezzie to move the family west. They arrived in Santa Barbara when Pearl was 11 years old.

Pearl's commitment to improving her hometown can be traced to her teen years. In 1907, while alighting from the train while on holiday from studies at Berkeley, she is said to have resolved to beautify Santa Barbara. From its early establishment as a mud fort, the city had evolved into a collection of adobe pueblos, Victorian frame and brick houses, and a mishmash of shabby buildings.

But first, Pearl turned her attention to public health.

After graduating summa cum laude from the University of California in 1909, Pearl returned to Santa Barbara and set her sights on an old slaughterhouse in the center of town. She organized a group of women who raised a ruckus about its odor and looks, and health officials closed it down.

Next, she went after the dairies, insisting they improve sanitation. She also led a fight to condemn the old county hospital and poor farm for their sanitary conditions. A new county medical facility was built west of the city because of her efforts.

During World War I, Pearl Chase founded the Santa Barbara chapter of the Red Cross and led food and book drives for soldiers.

Finally, in 1920, she began her crusade to change the face of Santa Barbara and transform it into the paradise it is today.

In that year, Miss Chase helped organize the Community Arts Association, and two years later, she and Mr. and Mrs. Bernhard Hoffmann founded the association's Plans and Planting Committee. This group began a campaign to make Spanish colonial architecture the city's dominant style, an effort that was vastly furthered by the devastating 1925 earthquake.

The quake shook most of the city to the ground. In its wake, Miss Chase and the committee persuaded the city to adopt the preferred style of architecture and appoint an architectural review board to ensure that the style was followed as the city was rebuilt.

From that time on, the committee, or, to be more accurate, Miss Chase, became a dominant voice in preservation and conservation efforts throughout Santa Barbara. Among her many victories, she argued for and won city architectural and zoning guidelines. She led a fight to ban billboards in Santa Barbara County and founded the Trust for Historic Preservation, which is restoring the site of the original Spanish presidio. She also assisted in the development of Santa Barbara City College's outstanding adult education program.

Over the years, Miss Chase helped establish many enduring traditions in the community, including the annual Old Spanish Days Fiesta (which was begun in 1924 to benefit the newly built Lobero Theatre); the Santa Barbara Indian Defense Association, which later became the National Association of American Indian Affairs, dedicated to furthering the cause of Native Americans; the Council of Christmas Cheer, one of the city's most successful charities, now called Christmas Unity; and many other civic and charitable organizations.

Miss Chase received two honorary doctorates—from UCSB and Mills College—as well as many other honors over the years. She never married; historians say she had no time.

When Miss Chase died in 1979, just before her 91st birthday, one eulogist wrote of her, "One wonders whether Pearl Chase will be satisfied with Heaven, after leaving her beloved Santa Barbara."

Pearl Chase's personal papers and photographs, a collection spanning 60 years, are housed at UCSB's Special Collections Library.

Casa Dorinda, a large estate that today is a retirement community for the wealthy. And there was Avery Brundage, a Chicago contractor who made millions, lost his fortune in the Depression, and then recovered it in real estate. Brundage owned the Montecito Country Club and the El Paseo building in downtown Santa Barbara in the 1950s.

These men and their families are typical of the people who brought wealth and, through their philanthropy and guidance, helped the community retain its charm and air of exclusivity. They also created a wide variety of cultural and civic organizations, far more than are usual in communities of Santa Barbara's size.

The presence of these influential Santa Barbarans has been a magnet for dignitaries. Presidents and royalty have vacationed or visited here. Rutherford B. Hayes and Benjamin Harrison paid visits in the 1800s. William McKinley, Teddy Roosevelt, and Herbert Hoover made campaign stops.

President John F. Kennedy and his bride, Jacqueline, honeymooned at the graceful San Ysidro Ranch in Montecito in 1953. His brother Robert and his wife, Ethel, also honeymooned here. President Ronald Reagan still retains his hilltop ranch just northwest of the city. During Reagan's presidency, from 1981 to 1989, Santa Barbara became known as the "western White House," and the flurry of media people and presidential aides that accompanied him put the city in the national spotlight throughout the decade. Soon after President Bill Clinton's election in 1992, he and his wife, Hillary, vacationed at the beachside estate of television producers Harry Thomason and Linda Bloodworth-Thomason.

Movie stars and entertainers continue to seek solace in Santa Barbara and Montecito. In earlier years, actors Ronald Colman, Leo Carrillo, and Rita Hayworth spent time here, as did Charlie Chaplin, who married a woman from the South Coast community of Carpinteria. More recently, Michael Douglas, Kevin Costner, Jonathan Winters, George Michael, Eva Marie Saint, Kenny Loggins, and Fess Parker have been among the many entertainers who have made the Santa Barbara area their home.

Queen Elizabeth II of England visited in 1983. She arrived during a major storm but managed to visit promi-nent spots in the city, including the Santa Barbara Mission, and made a treacherous trip up the mud-slick mountain road leading to the Reagan ranch to see the president and his wife.

Soviet Premier Nikita Khrushchev stopped here during his tour of the country in 1959, and former Soviet President Mikhail Gorbachev, who presided over the breakup of the Soviet Union in the late 1980s, has visited on several occasions.

GROWTH OF THE REGION

While celebrities and the wealthy have made Santa Barbara their playground, longtime residents like actor Michael Douglas, comedian Jonathan Winters, and musician Kenny Loggins have contributed to efforts that have benefited the less fortunate and enriched the arts.

Many others shared in the creation of the city. Thomas More Storke, father of the city's daily newspaper—the *News-Press*—guided the paper and the community through six decades. He founded the paper in 1901 and ran it until his retirement, at the age of 88, in 1964. During that time Storke helped bring about the creation of the University of California campus at Santa Barbara, persuaded the federal government to build a new postal building and to allow him to choose the architect who would design it (at considerably more cost than was budgeted), worked to get an airport established, championed the federal construction of Bradbury Dam and Lake Cachuma to provide water to the South Coast, and served briefly as an appointed U.S. senator.

Storke's overt power was matched by Pearl Chase's behind-the-scenes influence. Her involvement in the development of the city cannot be overstated. The Plans and Planting Committee, which she chaired from 1927 until the mid-1970s, created architectural and building guidelines still in force. Chase's presence was felt in many aspects of civic and cultural life and remains a guiding influence.

Chase's efforts also led to the founding of the Citizens Planning Association in 1960, still an important voice in the community, and to the adoption in 1964 of the City of Santa Barbara's first general plan. This planning document assessed the spurt of growth that had occurred along

THE LOBERO THEATRE, BUILT
in the early 1920s, is the site for
a variety of performing arts
events, including dramatic
presentations, dance recitals,
and screenings of films.

COMMERCIAL BUILDINGS along State Street reflect the Mediterranean architectural style found throughout El Pueblo Viejo, Santa Barbara's historic district downtown.

the South Coast since 1956, analyzed the reasons, and laid down a series of guidelines for future development that helped solidify the hard-won recommendations Chase had crafted for the city .

Establishment of the University of California at Santa Barbara in the mid-1950s, development of a source of water from newly built Lake Cachuma, and the statewide population explosion that spurred creation of the city general plan also brought much change to neighboring Goleta Valley.

Once a sleepy stretch of agricultural land to the west of Santa Barbara, the Goleta Valley is home to more than 80,000 people. With the city, it makes up the focal point of the greater Santa Barbara region known as the South Coast, housing more than 200,000 people. UCSB, the municipal airport, and the corporations that have helped create Santa Barbara's image as a home for high-tech industry are actually in the area known as Goleta.

The word *Goleta* is Spanish, derived from the Arabic word *galata*, for "schooner." Several hundred years ago, tall-masted schooners sailed the Santa Barbara Channel to trade in a small deep-water cove near what was then called Mescalitan Island. The earliest recorded schooner visit to the cove was that of Cabrillo, in 1542. The inlet was silted in by the 1860s and ultimately filled and graded to make way for what is now Santa Barbara Municipal Airport.

In the 1700s and 1800s, the cove was a vibrant trading place. Mescalitan Island was a favored shelter for schooners, particularly those trading in Pacific sea otter pelts, a lucrative commodity cherished by the Chinese.

Goleta's history is closely intertwined with Santa Barbara's. The Spanish-Mexican colonization of the coastline led to sweeping ranchos and adobes named for the men who settled the valley: W. W. Stow and his son, Sherman, who built the now-restored Stow House; and Daniel Hill, whose adobe home on La Patera Lane is the oldest home in the Goleta Valley.

Daniel Hill and his son-in-law, Nicholas Den, are credited with helping to preserve Santa Barbara Mission throughout the tumultuous years following secularization. In 1845, they offered to lease the mission and its

The county courthouse tower offers a spectacular 180-degree panoramic view of the city. Left, the Queen of the Missions, Santa Barbara's most famous structure.

holdings for $1,200 a year in gold. Devout Catholics, the two men had decided it was their duty to protect the mission from falling into the wrong hands, and the lease resulted in the mission's uninterrupted operation by the Franciscans through the establishment of California statehood in 1850.

Goleta, the largest unincorporated urban area in the state, grew up in the 1960s mostly as a suburb of Santa Barbara. Today, it is a vibrant community on its own.

Santa Barbara and the Goleta Valley share a vivid and dramatic history. Each has its own personality, as does each of the wonderful smaller communities that extend east and west along the coast. Each is unique, but, as parts of a whole, each also contributes to creating the essence of what is generally referred to as Paradise.

THE COUNTY COURTHOUSE (LEFT) IS
a favorite spot for couples to take their
wedding vows. Romantics also are drawn
to Stearns Wharf, which provides a
unique sunset view of the waterfront.

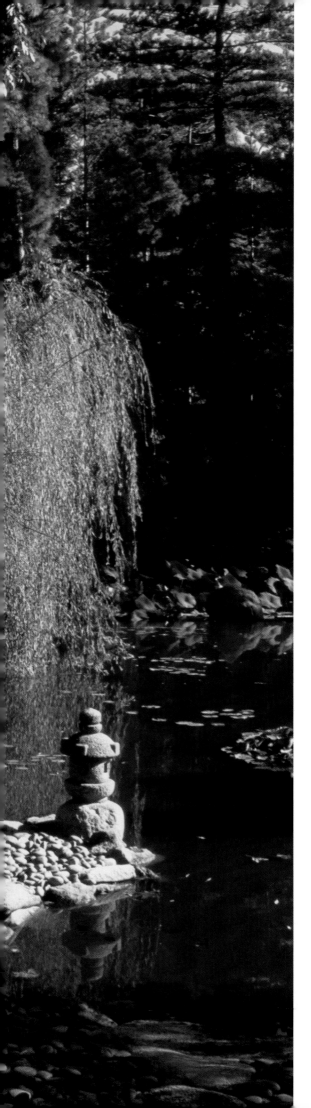

LOTUSLAND, A GARDEN
estate tucked away in Montecito,
was once the pride and joy of
Madame Ganna Walska, an eccentric opera singer with a penchant
for marrying wealthy men. The
stunning estate is now owned by a
nonprofit organization dedicated to
preserving and enhancing the gardens through educational tours.

SOUTH COAST COMMUNITIES

ALTHOUGH THE ENTIRE SOUTH COAST REGION IS GENERALLY REFERRED TO AS SANTA BARBARA, THE AREA IS ACTUALLY MADE UP OF SEVERAL COMMUNITIES: GOLETA AND ISLA VISTA TO THE WEST OF THE CITY AND MONTECITO, SUMMERLAND, AND CARPINTERIA (ALSO AN INCORPORATED CITY) TO THE EAST. EACH OF THESE TOWNS HAS ITS OWN DISTINCT PERSONALITY, WHILE COMPLEMENTING THE CITY OF SANTA BARBARA.

Santa Barbara is the crown jewel in the array of gemstones that comprise the South Coast. Urban in character, the city is upscale and low-key at the same time. It is a diverse community; about a quarter of its residents are Latino. Although many can trace their heritage to the establishment of the presidio, others immigrated in recent years from Mexico and other Latin American countries.

Santa Barbarans have a reputation for being concerned and involved in everything from schools and politics to charitable and cultural activities. They also are outdoor enthusiasts, and the natural environment makes for a wonderful year-round playground.

The region's south-facing beaches are unique on the Pacific Coast. From Alaska to South America, the ocean slaps against the continent from the west, but for 70 miles along the South Coast, the waves come from the south. The Channel Islands 25 miles offshore protect the mainland from storms, as do the mountains to the north of the city. Thus, the region is blessed with soft, warm breezes and mild temperatures throughout most of the year. The city is often called the American Riviera.

The beaches and ocean are natural focal points for residents and visitors alike. Stearns Wharf and the city's marina and working harbor are tourist attractions as well as commercial powerhouses.

Stearns Wharf, at the base of the city's main thoroughfare, State Street, was built in 1871. A lumberman by the name of John Peck Stearns convinced the city to build the wharf so his ships could unload logs onto a dock instead of floating them ashore. Today, the wharf is home to a seafood store, restaurants, and souvenir shops as well as the Sea Center, a museum of ocean life owned by the Santa Barbara Natural History Museum.

On Sundays, the city's Arts and Crafts Festival dominates Cabrillo Boulevard, which fronts the city's beaches. Local artisans sell their wares along a mile of Chase Palm Park stretching east of the wharf. Browsers and buyers can find paintings, photographs, and a vast array of crafts created exclusively by Santa Barbara County residents.

A little west of the wharf, the Santa Barbara Harbor and Breakwater provide shelter for pleasure craft as well as the city's commercial fishing fleet. At the end of the day, visitors can often watch the fishing boats unload their catches—a panoply of seafood from local waters that may include urchins, halibut, thresher shark, and salmon. On Saturday mornings, the harbor becomes a fresh fish market where early risers can buy seafood right off the boats.

Saturday mornings are also the occasion for the city's long-running Certified Farmers Market. Held in a city parking lot at Santa Barbara and Cota Streets, the market is a weekly gathering at which one is as likely to find political activists and street musicians as fresh vegetables. Many residents wouldn't think of missing it. Organic fruits, honey, nuts, and other locally grown produce and fresh flowers are available from 8:30 A.M. until noon. A second farmers market occupies several blocks of Lower State Street every Tuesday from late afternoon till dusk.

Santa Barbara's natural beauty makes the city an ideal setting for a wide variety of festivals and celebrations throughout the year.

In March, the Santa Barbara International Film Festival draws visitors from all over the world to view the best new and unusual films of the year. The festival has grown in reputation and offerings and is a major highlight of the winter season.

From April through October, the city sponsors a series of cultural and ethnic festivals at Oak Park. The Jewish Festival kicks off these weekend-long events. Over the summer, other festivals celebrate Chinese, Irish, French, Greek, Italian, Mexican, and German cultures. One festival is dedicated exclusively to the city's children.

Over Memorial Day weekend, I Madonnari is held at the old mission. An Italian sidewalk chalk-painting festival and arts and crafts show, this annual event benefits a nonprofit arts organization called the Children's Creative Project.

In June, the city puts on a most unusual celebration: the Summer Solstice Parade. It was begun by a few

Santa Barbarans love to be outdoors, whether bicycling at Stearns Wharf or enjoying events like the Solstice Parade (right) each June.

held on the beach at the base of Stearns Wharf and features the best of the region's jazz musicians, as well as well-known bands from New Orleans and other major jazz venues.

While all the festivals make for a lot of fun, Santa Barbara does have its serious side. Its residents support hundreds of local charities and arts organizations through vast donations of time and money and thus contribute to making the city's cultural and art offerings unmatched in variety and quality. Several hundred charities operate here, from nationally known groups like United Way to several, like Fighting Back, that are unique to Santa Barbara.

Fighting Back was organized by a woman named Penny Jenkins in the late 1980s to combat drug and alcohol abuse in the community. Jenkins, executive director of the Santa Barbara Council on Alcoholism and Drug Abuse, brought together community leaders and created a "fighting back" plan that won a multimillion-dollar grant from the Robert Wood Johnson Foundation.

When one begins to talk of contributions, the discussion must be broadened to include people from the region—not just the city. The residents of the entire South Coast—from the Goleta Valley on the west to Carpinteria at the eastern edge—contribute enormously to making the area a civic as well as a cultural paradise.

GOLETA

Goleta is the largest of Santa Barbara's satellite communities. It stretches from the western boundary of the city to Winchester Canyon, which marks the outer fringes of development along the South Coast. Included in this area is Isla Vista, an oceanside enclave that is home to many students who attend the University of California at Santa Barbara.

Isla Vista is notorious for its history of protest and partying. In 1970, the Bank of America branch there was burned to the ground by student protesters. Much to the chagrin of University of California officials and the residents of the South Coast, the community is best

friends who decided to celebrate the solstice one year by dancing down State Street. The parade, which draws more than 80,000 people each June, is unique in that no mechanical contraptions or marching bands are allowed, and there are no equestrians or floats in the traditional sense. Rather, the "floats" consist of costumes and getups created by the parade participants and, depending on the theme of the day, can range from giant papier-mâché zoo animals to a seascape featuring a 12-foot inflatable squid. The result is pure artistic whimsy.

For 10 days in early July, the city hosts the annual Semana Nautica Sports Festival. Amateur athletes come from all over the world to compete in events such as lifeguard championships, a triathlon, jet-ski races, and a three-mile ocean swim.

In the first week of August, the city celebrates its heritage with the annual Old Spanish Days Fiesta. It is essentially a four-day party, during which residents enjoy parades, nightly shows of dance and music, two *mercados*, or marketplaces, where one can find every imaginable example of Mexican cuisine, and parties galore.

Over Labor Day weekend, the International Jazz Festival puts the city in a musical mood. The festival is

PENNY JENKINS FIGHTS BACK

Penny Jenkins moved to Santa Barbara with little inkling of the impact she would have on the community. A mother of three, she had lived all over the world, owned a successful design firm in the Southwest, and logged many volunteer hours with various organizations.

Soon after relocating to Santa Barbara, Jenkins joined the board of the Council on Alcoholism and Drug Abuse. Just a few months later, she was asked to become the council's director. When she took over, the council had seven employees, a budget of $180,000, and was $30,000 in the red. She immediately began a fund-raising effort to get the organization back on solid footing.

But she didn't stop there. She began to recognize that Santa Barbara may be a paradise, but like every other community, it had unmistakable—though perhaps undiscussed—drug and alcohol abuse problems.

In the early 1990s, Jenkins heard about a special $3 million grant offered by the Robert Wood Johnson Foundation. Eight communities around the nation would be given the money to formulate innovative programs to fight drug and alcohol abuse. But the winning groups would have to show a community-wide commitment and develop a proposal the foundation deemed feasible and worthy of funding.

Over the course of several months, Jenkins enlisted the resources and commitment of dozens of community leaders. She formed a 50-member task force and separate steering and program development committees. They named the effort Fighting Back, and it so impressed the Robert Wood Johnson Foundation that Fighting Back was awarded a $200,000 two-year planning grant. The result was the development of a community program that won the final $3 million grant and that has made measurable strides in the battle against alcoholism and drug abuse in Santa Barbara.

So successful has the program been that in the summer of 1995, the steering committee voted to continue Fighting Back by seeking alternative funding sources after the grant is over.

Today, Jenkins presides over an organization that employs more than 50 people and operates with a $2.5 million annual budget. Out of Fighting Back's efforts have come plans to tackle other concerns, such as gangs.

Jenkins has won numerous honors for her steadfast commitment and tireless efforts on behalf of Fighting Back and other council programs. She was named Woman of the Year in 1993 by the Santa Barbara Ad Club. The new building purchased by local benefactors for Fighting Back's headquarters was named for her. She was the first woman invited to join the Santa Barbara Rotary Club.

Life has certainly brought change and new experiences for Jenkins. A competitive skier who grew up in Great Falls, Montana, she went to the University of Colorado to study and ski. But she married the captain of the football team in her sophomore year and left school to raise a family.

Over the years, Jenkins moved frequently because of her husband's business. Nonetheless, she managed to earn degrees in business and public administration and to become deeply involved with the Junior League, various community councils on alcoholism and drug abuse, the PTA, and other charitable organizations.

Jenkins first became interested in alcoholism and drug abuse while doing graduate work. Touched by a neighbor's struggle with the disease, she did her master's thesis on the subject. She could not have known how much it would affect her life, in tragic and uplifting ways.

In 1982, her daughter Lisa, then 17 years old, was involved in a car accident late one night after drinking with friends. Lisa was so traumatized by the accident that she came home and shot herself. Jenkins found her daughter's body in the vault of their Scottsdale, Arizona, estate.

Seeking understanding, Jenkins went back to school to study psychology, which led to her earning another master's degree from Antioch University.

In a letter to the Robert Wood Johnson Foundation, Jenkins once wrote: "Life has taught me lessons which one cannot learn in school—the ability to understand, communicate with, persuade and motivate, and inspire diverse groups of individuals to work together in pursuit of a common goal."

That is indeed what Jenkins has done, and through her efforts, the people of the South Coast have reaped enormous benefits.

NOCHES DE RONDA, DURING
the city's annual Fiesta, draws
crowds to the Sunken Gardens
at the county courthouse for
nighttime dancing and music
(left). La Presidente Ellen Harte
(above) led the 1995 celebration.

Kid's World, Santa Barbara's most elaborate playground, was built by more than 4,000 volunteers during four days in 1993. At left is a typical church tower in the city.

favored gathering spot, since residents must pick up their mail there.

Summerland is a favorite spot for antique hunters. The town has numerous antique shops, as well as restaurants and gift boutiques.

Summerland was founded in 1879 as a colony for spiritualists, who were said to practice channeling and other "spooky" things. In fact, for a time the nearby townspeople called Summerland "Spookville." The name disappeared, as did the oil production that fueled the community's economy in the late 1800s.

Oil production was common along the South Coast in those early years. Summerland and Carpinteria were oil and tar production venues, as was Goleta. The Santa Barbara Channel contains vast reservoirs of oil, and in the late nineteenth century, natural seeps of the thick gooey substance drew black gold prospectors to

the area. Oil production along the coast continues today, though under very different circumstances.

Early photographs of the Summerland shoreline show dozens of oil wells operating at the water's edge. Strip mining for tar, or natural asphaltum, along the Carpinteria coast occurred from 1875 to the early 1920s. Today, the beaches are free of oil production equipment, but state and federal waters offshore contain derricks that continue to pump out millions of barrels of crude each year.

CARPINTERIA

Carpinteria, the farthest east of the South Coast communities, is an incorporated city, like Santa Barbara. Considered a Santa Barbara suburb, Carpinteria boasts the "world's safest beach." Whether the safest or not, it is one of the broadest and most attractive of the

OUTFITTED IN TRADITIONAL
silver-studded gear, a participant
in the Fiesta Parade struts down
State Street during the annual
August event. Flower girls are in
abundance at many events and
activities throughout Fiesta week.

FOLLOWING PAGES
The Cold Spring Arch Bridge,
leading to the Santa Ynez
Valley, is one of the longest
arch-span bridges in the country
and has been described as the
most beautiful.

South Coast's sandy stretches and lends a funky beach-town atmosphere to Carpinteria's downtown. Linden Avenue, the primary commercial strip, goes straight down to the ocean from Highway 101. Antique shops, retail stores, and burger joints dot the avenue. But avocados and cut flowers grown in greenhouses generate a good portion of the local economy.

Avocados are especially important to the community. In September, the city celebrates their value with a three-day Avocado Festival, which draws tens of thousands of people to the town. Festival-goers can taste-test avocado ice cream and other foods made from this unusual green fruit.

SANTA YNEZ VALLEY

No discussion of Paradise would be complete without mentioning the Santa Ynez Valley, although technically it is not part of the South Coast. Just 24 miles over the mountains north of Santa Barbara, the valley is a bucolic getaway where vineyards and wineries co-exist with ranchers and horse breeders. Here also is Lake Cachuma, a federally operated reservoir created in the 1950s with the construction of Bradbury Dam. The lake is a year-round recreation area but is noted for the large number of pairs of bald eagles that nest there. Boat tours provide an opportunity to observe the eagles and other rare and endangered animals living at the lake.

There are several communities throughout the valley. Among the best known is Solvang, the self-described Danish capital of the country. Its village atmosphere—with its Danish-style shops and windmills—is a major tourist attraction, while reflecting the community's roots.

The town was founded in 1911 by a group of Danish educators who wanted to establish a college and colony. The community, which remains mostly Danish, celebrates its history each year in late September with Danish Days. Fresh Danish pastries, dancing, a parade, and other entertainment are featured. Any time of the year, though, visitors can enjoy melt-in-the-mouth pastries, shop along quaint village streets, and feel almost as if they were transported to Copenhagen.

West and east of Solvang are the towns of Buellton and Santa Ynez, respectively. Buellton, located at the conjunction of Highways 101 and 246, is home to Pea Soup Andersen's restaurant, where its famous split pea soup is a hearty choice of travelers. Santa Ynez is a tiny community that rests on its frontier roots. Its three-block downtown is a replica of an Old West town.

Farther north of Santa Ynez, along Highway 154, is the small town of Los Olivos. This charming community is made up of Victorian and western-style buildings but has become known in recent years for its art galleries. It is home to Mattei's Tavern, which served as a major stagecoach stop from the late 1800s through the turn of the century. Mattei's Tavern continues to serve travelers, who can find evidence of the valley's history in the photographs and memorabilia in the restaurant.

Throughout the valley are some of the best vintners in the state and, arguably, the world. Since the late 1960s, when Boyd Bettencourt decided to plant some grape vines on his dairy's pasture land, wine making has been a major industry. Bettencourt's Santa Ynez Valley Winery was inspired by the boom in Northern California's Napa and Sonoma Valleys. Since then, more than 30 wineries have opened. Bettencourt and others discovered that the Santa Ynez Valley offers a near-perfect climate and geographic setting for wine grapes.

Sparse rain, warm days, cool evenings, and the nighttime fog that drifts in over the mountain range to the south combine to make for an especially good growing area. Wine makers have won particular praise for the chardonnays and pinot noirs that are produced here. Cabernet sauvignon and sauvignon blanc grapes also make superior wines.

The wineries are sprinkled throughout the valley and range from large corporate-owned vintners like Zaca Mesa Winery near Los Olivos to small growers like Au Bon Climat, Houtz, and Qupe. Most of the wineries offer tastings or tours for visitors. A day spent wine tasting in the valley is sure to be extremely enjoyable. The scenery is spectacular, the tasting rooms are often situated against a backdrop of mountains and vineyards, and many wineries offer picnic areas.

THREE

CULTURE AND THE ARTS

ANTA BARBARA HAS OFTEN BEEN CALLED A MECCA FOR THE ARTS. OVER THE YEARS, MANY THOUSANDS OF PATRONS AND GENEROUS BENEFACTORS HAVE HELPED MAKE THE CHOICES IN BOTH THE PERFORMING AND VISUAL ARTS BROAD AND VARIED—INDEED, FAR MORE EXTENSIVE THAN IS TYPICAL OF A CITY ITS SIZE.

*R*esidents of the South Coast, as well as visitors to the area, can choose from an extensive array of museums, concerts, plays, dance performances, and university-sponsored lectures, films, and other special events. More than 85 organizations, including the University of California at Santa Barbara, Westmont College in Montecito, and Santa Barbara City College, are devoted to bringing top-notch performing and visual arts to the region.

Theaters such as the fabulous Arlington and the historic Lobero provide venues for orchestral performances, plays, films, and concerts, while the Granada is home to the highly successful Santa Barbara Civic Light Opera.

The Music Academy of the West attracts students from all over the world to its summer instructional sessions, and the Community Arts Music Association sponsors performances by international touring orchestras. The Santa Barbara Symphony is renowned as one of the finest small-city symphonies. Established in 1953, it is led today by Gisele Ben-Dor, the orchestra's first woman conductor.

Dance enthusiasts can choose from a range of groups, including the Santa Barbara Festival Ballet, Santa Barbara Dance Theatre, Santa Barbara Chamber Ballet, and Santa Barbara Dance Warehouse.

The Santa Barbara Museum of Art, UCSB's art museum, and the Contemporary Arts Forum (CAF) help maintain a vibrant environment for visual artists that is furthered by numerous private galleries.

The region's theater groups include the fabulous Ensemble Theatre Company at the Alhecama Theatre, the Access Theatre, Theatre UCSB and UCSB's Theater Artists Group, Westmont's Theater Department, and the Santa Barbara City College Theatre Group. And for those looking to see new and unusual dramatic productions, there are Dramatic Women and the Slightly Askew Players.

A short way up the coast, the Circle Bar B Guest Ranch offers fun and rollicking dinner theater on Refugio Canyon Road in the mountains near Gaviota. In Solvang, the Pacific Conservatory of the Performing Arts Theatrefest stages productions in a theater under the stars. It is an experience well worth the drive over the mountains.

In short, there is little missing in the way of the cultural arts in Santa Barbara.

MUSEUMS

The Santa Barbara Museum of Art is one of the community's great jewels. Originally the site of the city's post office, the building at 1130 State Street was remodeled and converted into the Museum of Art in 1941. In 1983, a major addition was constructed on the southeast side of the building, providing an entrance and connection to the paseo that connects to La Arcada Court and the Santa Barbara Public Library. The museum houses permanent collections of Asian, European, and American art, as well as contemporary photography. Throughout the year touring exhibits bring new artworks to the community.

In late 1995, the museum announced a $5.1 million expansion that will add a 13,000-square-foot wing to the main building on State Street. By project's end, the museum will boast three new or renovated galleries, an enlarged gift shop and cafe at street level, a graphics study center, and additional art storage space.

If the Museum of Art offers a classical view of art, then the Santa Barbara Contemporary Arts Forum could be considered its alter ego. The Contemporary Arts Forum was founded in 1976 by a group of artists and others interested in bringing top-quality contemporary art to Santa Barbara. In the early years, the museum existed in temporary spaces, but in 1981, it found a permanent home in the Balboa Building on State Street. In 1990, the CAF was moved into new gallery space in the Paseo Nuevo mall downtown.

Since the gallery's founding, its exhibits have been at the vanguard of the contemporary arts movement. CAF offers works by local, regional, national, and international artists 15 to 20 times a year. Its focus is on enhancing the understanding of contemporary artworks in the context of their reflections on and of society. Bold and provocative, CAF installations always provide food for thought and discussion. To that end, the museum often stages other events—for example, lectures, video programs, performances, and classes for artists—in conjunction with its exhibits.

One of the unusual features of CAF is its organizational structure. Two committees—one for exhibits and one for performances—meet each month to decide on the installations that will be brought in and on programs. A strong commitment to bringing art into the community has resulted in several exhibits being staged off-site.

The University Art Museum, on the UCSB campus, displays contemporary art as well as exhibits focusing on various artistic periods. Its permanent collection houses works from the fifteenth through the seventeenth centuries, including Renaissance plaquettes and medals from the Morgenroth Collection and paintings from the Sedgwick Collection. Throughout the year, the museum hosts lectures, panel discussions, and other special events.

Santa Barbara's Historical Society operates two museums. Its main museum, at the corner of de la Guerra and Santa Barbara Streets downtown, includes the Gledhill Library. Displays help visitors trace the region's history from the early Chumash period through Spanish colonialism and Mexican governance on up to modern times. One of its more stunning exhibits re-creates the city's Chinatown, which existed near the site of the old presidio from the late 1800s through the early 1900s. A large, ornate altar carved and encrusted with dragons and other intricate designs is spectacular.

The historical society also operates the Fernald House museum and the adjacent Trussell-Winchester Adobe. The Fernald House, named for Judge Charles and Hannah Hobbs Fernald, was built in the 1800s and is considered the city's finest example of Victorian architecture. Originally on Santa Barbara Street, the Fernald House was acquired by the historical society in 1959 and moved to its present location at 414 West Montecito Street that year. The Fernald House museum and the adjacent adobe are open on Sundays from 2:00 to 4:00 P.M.

The Santa Barbara Museum of Natural History is another South Coast treasure. An architecturally distinct building of Spanish colonial style, it is tucked into a grove of oaks along the creek in Mission Canyon. The museum houses the area's only planetarium and observatory, as well as exhibits on regional geology, Chumash history, marine life, and native plant and wildlife.

A 72-foot skeleton of a blue whale greets visitors at the entrance to the museum. Blue whales are a frequent sight in the Santa Barbara Channel during migration months. This particular creature washed up

The Santa Barbara Museum of Natural History (page 52) features exhibits on the Chumash way of life (above). Opposite, the Italian Street Chalk-Painting Festival, held each Memorial Day weekend.

on a local beach in the early 1980s. Scientists and researchers meticulously studied and methodically stripped the carcass, then rebuilt the skeleton on the museum grounds. The skeleton offers a good sense of the size and scale of these gentle giants of the deep. It is an impressive sight.

More common in channel waters are gray whales. Museum scientists have compiled one of the most complete studies of gray whale sightings—more than 1,800 since 1975—and their migration patterns.

The natural history museum also owns and operates the Sea Center on Stearns Wharf, which receives more than 70,000 visitors each year. Visitors can touch sea creatures in a re-created tide pool, take a video tour of underwater ocean life around the Channel Islands, and learn about the marine animals that populate local waters.

Santa Barbara also is home to some especially unusual museums, including the Karpeles Manuscript Library Museum. Founded by a Montecito couple in the early 1980s, it has tens of thousands of original historical documents and manuscripts that bring the past to life. The museum has two branches on the South Coast—one in Montecito and one in Santa Barbara—and five others around the country.

GRA

SANTA BARBARA CIVIC

WEST SIDE S

SPONSORED BY PA

The bird sanctuary exhibit at the Museum of Natural History is a favorite with visitors.

The South Coast Railroad Museum and Stow House on Los Carneros Road in Goleta are operated by the Goleta Valley Historical Society. The Railroad Museum features the authentic Goleta Depot, which was moved from its original location on Kellogg Avenue and is now restored. Stow House was built in the 1800s by W. W. Stow, an early and influential settler of the Goleta Valley. The two historic structures and surrounding grounds are the site of an annual Fourth of July community picnic, as well as other special events throughout the year.

The Santa Barbara Carriage and Western Arts Museum also offers a glimpse into the 1800s. It boasts one of the largest collections of antique horse-drawn carriages, including stage coaches and a fire pumper. The museum also has a large exhibit of western saddles and tack, much of it encrusted with silver, and a 123-foot frieze drawn by the famous western artist Edward Borein, who lived in Santa Barbara in the 1930s and early '40s. The museum is owned by the Old Spanish Days organization, which stages Santa Barbara's annual Fiesta. Many of the carriages are featured in El Desfile Historico, the Fiesta Parade.

THEATERS

There is no question that the South Coast's most valuable and interesting theater, from a historical point of view, is the Arlington. Built on the site of what was originally the posh Arlington Hotel, the theater was erected in 1930-31 by the Fox West Coast Theatres as a movie house in which to showcase the film company's newest productions.

The original Arlington Hotel, built in an Italianate style, burned to the ground in 1909 and was replaced with a four-story structure of mission revival-style architecture. The second hotel was badly damaged in the 1925 earthquake, leading the Fox Theatres to investigate using it as a site for a new theater. The story goes that Joseph Plunkett, who was a driving force behind the remake of Santa Barbara in the Spanish colonial style, asked for a meeting with Fox officials. He so impressed them with a sketched drawing of the theater that, on the spot, Fox commissioned

The Santa Barbara Museum of Art is a lovely spot for a variety of events, including this Chinese New Year celebration.

Plunkett's firm, Edwards and Plunkett, to design it. Though the full plans were never realized, the theater is a stunningly beautiful structure, with a tall spire and long arched courtyard that links the theater to State Street. And as exquisite as the building's exterior is architecturally, the interior is as impressive. Inside, the theater walls depict a Spanish village, and graceful balconies overlook the stage. The deep-blue ceiling looks like a beautiful night sky, with twinkling star lights.

The Arlington Theatre is owned by Metropolitan Theaters and remains in use as a movie theater. It also is the home of the Santa Barbara Symphony, as well as a venue for other performing arts events throughout the year. It was designated a city landmark in 1975.

Another famous Santa Barbara theater is the Lobero. The oldest continuously operating theater in California, the Lobero was built in 1873 and originally used as an opera house. In 1924, the well-known Santa Barbara architect George Washington Smith, along with Lutah Maria Riggs, designed the present structure in the Spanish

colonial style. Today, the theater is operated by the private Lobero Foundation, which launched a four-year renovation project in 1993.

The theater also serves as a performing arts center for the community, offering everything from films to dramas, dance performances, and musical productions. The Lobero is home to the Santa Barbara Chamber Orchestra, the Contemporary Music Theater, the Grand Opera, and the Santa Barbara Festival Ballet. The theater was the first home of the Civic Light Opera, which moved in the early 1990s to the more spacious Granada Theater.

The Granada Theater is also owned by Metropolitan Theaters and at one time was used regularly for movie screenings. (Construction of the eight-story Granada Building during 1922–24 prompted the adoption in 1924 of a city ordinance limiting all future commercial buildings to no more than six stories and residential buildings to three stories.) During its production season, the Civic Light Opera takes the stage and transforms the Granada into a place where theatergoers can see first-rate Broadway musicals.

A MUSEUM THAT INSTILLS HOPE

One of the most fascinating museums in Santa Barbara is the Karpeles Manuscript Library Museum. The museum, which has the world's largest private holding of original historical documents and manuscripts, contains the original draft proposal for the U.S. Bill of Rights and documents written by such scientific greats as Darwin, Galileo, Newton, and Einstein.

Founders David and Marsha Karpeles have dedicated this phenomenal collection to "the preservation of the Original writings of the Great Authors, Scientists, Philosophers, Statesmen, Sovereigns and Leaders from All the Periods of World History."

The collection also includes the original proposal for the Apollo Lunar Landing Project and other documents from man's first wanderings into space. It holds the only known separate page of the first printing of the Ten Commandments from the Gutenberg Bible. The Emancipation Proclamation amendment to the Constitution, signed by Abraham Lincoln, is included, as are pages from Charles Darwin's handwritten manuscripts for *The Origin of the Species and The Descent of Man*.

The library's documents are both awe-inspiring and educational.

David Karpeles, in a letter explaining his motivation for creating the collection, wrote that he feared for American children, who grow up today without a sense of destiny and thus hope for the future. Karpeles believes an examination of history, literature, and the great accomplishments of science, government, art, and music can instill that hope.

"Our children . . . do not know who is Simon Bolivar, Rudyard Kipling, Immanuel Kant, Franklin Pierce, Sir Walter Raleigh, Virginia Dare or Queen Isabella. They are hardly aware of the Quest for the Indies, *The Origin of the Species*, the discovery of vaccines, the Reformation, the Black Plague, Esperanto, the *Peer Gynt Suites*, the *Rubaiyat*, the Magna Carta," Karpeles writes.

"It is to cure this lack and thereby fulfill my own desire to renew the sense of purpose for our children and ourselves that the Karpeles Manuscript Library has been created."

Karpeles, once a math teacher at Westmont College in Montecito, opened the original branch of the library in 1983.

Today, the Karpeles collection is housed in seven locations nationwide, including in the original library in Montecito, at 430 Hot Springs Road, and at 21 West Anapamu Street in downtown Santa Barbara. The other branches are in Tacoma, Washington; Jacksonville, Florida; Duluth, Minnesota; Buffalo, New York; and Charleston, South Carolina.

Most of the libraries have ongoing programs with area schools and colleges, so that schoolchildren and scholars alike have access to some of the most valuable documents in the world. The libraries are open to the public, and admission is free.

Documents and artifacts from the U.S. and Soviet space programs are among the historical treasures at the downtown Santa Barbara Karpeles Manuscript Library Museum. At right are the museum's founders, David and Marsha Karpeles.

Ludington Court in the Museum of Art features fine marble statuary.

Other theaters that offer top-quality drama include the Alhecama, home to the Ensemble Theatre Company; the Center Stage Theatre at Paseo Nuevo; the Garvin Theater at Santa Barbara City College; Westmont's Porter Theatre; and the Hatlen, Girvetz, and Studio Theaters at UCSB.

The Alhecama is a cozy theater tucked behind the Playa Azul Cafe on Santa Barbara Street. Originally built as a dance and acting studio, it was known as the Pueblo Theater until 1940, when Alice F. Schott purchased the property and renamed it Alhecama, a compilation of the first two letters of her daughters' names: Alice, Helen, Catherine, and Mary Lou.

In 1946, Alice Schott donated the land on which the theater stood for use as the headquarters for what would become Santa Barbara City College's adult education program. The adult education program outgrew the complex and sold it in 1981. Since then, the resident Ensemble Theatre Company has received wide praise for its award-winning productions of both the new and the classical and for its casts, a brilliant blend of professional and local actors.

Of special note is Access Theatre, an innovative theater group that stages productions that incorporate actors who have disabilities. Every performance is signed in American Sign Language, and many of the themes of the plays have to do with being differently abled in today's society.

Access Theatre was founded by its creative director, Rod Lathim, in 1979. At the time, Lathim has said, the idea of bringing theater to disabled people as well as showcasing the talents of disabled actors was not popular. Lathim persisted, however, and the theater group has won high praise over the years both locally and nationally.

Storm Reading, written and acted by Neal Marcus in the early 1990s, was one of its most successful productions. Marcus has dystonia, a rare neurological disease characterized by seizures and spasms, and the play is a series of vignettes based on his experiences. A national tour brought Marcus wide acclaim for his acting skills. In addition, the United Nations Society of Writers bestowed on him a literary award and medal of excellence for playwriting.

Access Theatre continues to produce some of the most progressive theater today. Area celebrities, most notably actor Michael Douglas, have contributed time and money over the years to keeping the vision for Access Theatre alive.

MUSIC

Music has been an integral part of the cultural arts in Santa Barbara for decades. The organizations involved range from the 77-year-old Community Arts Music Association (CAMA), which brings international symphony productions to the South Coast, to the infant Santa Barbara Grand Opera Association.

CAMA has been responsible for exposing Santa Barbara audiences to such distinguished music groups as

THE FRENCH GALLERY AT the Museum of Art attracts visitors year-round.

FOR YEARS, THE HISTORIC
Mural Room at the Santa
Barbara County Courthouse was
the meeting place of the county
board of supervisors.

THE CIVIC LIGHT OPERA brings Broadway musicals to Santa Barbara, including this recent production of *Jesus Christ Superstar.*

THE SANTA BARBARA
Symphony is the *grande
dame* of the community's
orchestras.

Russia's St. Petersburg Philharmonic, the Dresden Staatskapelle, and the Hong Kong Philharmonic. CAMA has also sponsored performances by fine domestic orchestras, such as the Los Angeles Philharmonic and the St. Louis Symphony Orchestra.

The Grand Opera began in 1993 with an acclaimed production of *Die Fledermaus*. Audiences were wowed again in 1994 by *Hansel and Gretel* and in 1995 by *La Traviata*. The 1995–96 season included *Amahl and the Night Visitors* and *Carmen*. Such inspired beginnings promise many years of successful Grand Opera productions to come.

The Santa Barbara Symphony is without doubt the *grande dame* of the community's orchestras. It has existed for decades but was transformed into one of the finest symphonies of its kind during the 1980s under the directorship of Varujan Kojian. When Kojian died unexpectedly in March 1993, the community was stunned. Kojian had held the job for nine years and is widely credited with turning a small-town symphony into a world-class orchestra.

In June 1994, the board announced its choice of a new musical director: 39-year-old Gisele Ben-Dor, who is mesmerizing audiences with her selections and her skill.

Ben-Dor was born in Uruguay but emigrated to Israel in 1973. There she began her formal education in conducting. Ultimately, she studied and worked with such masters as Zubin Mehta and Leonard Bernstein. She was invited to conduct in Europe, then moved to the United States in the 1980s. In addition to the Santa Barbara Symphony, Ben-Dor is director of the Annapolis Symphony and Boston's ProArte Chamber Orchestra.

The South Coast is home to many other music organizations, including the Santa Barbara Chamber Orchestra, the Santa Barbara Choral Society, and the Santa Barbara Oratorio Chorale. The Santa Barbara Men's and Women's Ensemble elevates the human voice to pure instrument with its a cappella performances.

The Bach Camerata presents moving concerts featuring the chamber music of Bach, Beethoven, Handel, Mozart, and many other composers in productions staged at Lehmann Hall at the Music Academy of the West in Montecito and in the communities of Ventura and Thousand Oaks.

The Santa Barbara Chamber and Festival Ballets satisfy the passion for classical dance and music combined. Several private ballet companies round out the classical dance offerings. Dance Warehouse, Dance Alliance, and Dance for Every Body offer varied forms of human expression through dance, as do many productions sponsored by the UCSB Arts & Lectures Series throughout the academic year.

UCSB Arts & Lectures and the drama and music departments of Westmont College and Santa Barbara City College truly enrich the already stunning range of arts offerings.

In the 1995–96 season alone, UCSB Arts & Lectures sponsored performances by the San Francisco Mime Troupe, the Limon Dance Company, the Juilliard String Quartet, the Dancers and Musicians of Bali, the political comedy troupe the Capital Steps, and the Toronto Dance Theatre, among others.

No discussion of music in Santa Barbara would be complete without mention of the Music Academy of the West. Although perhaps not as famous as Interlochen and Ravinia, Santa Barbara's Music Academy of the West is recognized among those in the music world as on a par with the more well-known summer music institutes.

The finest music students from around the world arrive each summer to spend eight weeks learning with the masters. Santa Barbara is the true beneficiary, because the academy opens its master classes to the public and offers both student and faculty concerts throughout the season. Its faculty includes some of the finest instrumentalists and singers in the country, many of whom return year after year to teach their art to promising young musicians.

The great soprano Marilyn Horne, who studied under Lotte Lehmann at the academy more than 40 years ago, returned to teach voice for the summer of 1995, and in 1997, she will become the academy's full-time voice director. Many other faculty have long tenures or connections with the academy. Pianist Jerome Lowenthal, for example, has been with the institute for more than 25 years.

The academy's roots reach back to before the Second World War, when scientists, intellectuals, musicians,

A Chinese dragon jousts with a jester during a New Year's celebration.

and other artists from Europe sought refuge in the United States. The war years brought more exiles from Europe, many of whom settled in Southern California. The magnificent Lotte Lehmann came to Santa Barbara and is credited with inspiring some of the biggest names in music and philanthropy to establish the Music Academy.

Lehmann is said to have wanted Santa Barbara to become a "festival city, similar to Salzburg." Others shared the dream. Otto Klemperer, who had fled Nazi Germany and been director of the Los Angeles Philharmonic, was at the first meeting to discuss founding the academy. The great industrial magnate Max Fleischmann, a Montecito resident, helped form a committee to guide the effort. Actors Ronald Colman, Nelson Eddy, and Jeanette MacDonald, heiress Amy Du Pont, movie mogul Darryl Zanuck, and novelist Raymond Chandler contributed sizable donations for the effort.

The academy opened in July 1947 at the site of the Cate School in Carpinteria. The first summer's faculty included such luminaries in the music world as composer Ernest Bloch, pianist and teacher Harry Kaufmann, tenor

Richard Bonelli, conductor Richard Lert, violinist Roman Totenberg, and the members of the Griller String Quartet of England.

Lotte Lehmann and other eminent names in music formed the advisory board for the academy's first season.

In 1951, the executor of the estate of Mr. and Mrs. John Percival Jefferson announced that the Jeffersons' fabulous Miraflores estate in Montecito would be donated to the academy for a permanent home. Everything was set.

In 1953, Lehmann retired from the stage and joined the academy staff, serving as voice director until 1962. The great conductor Maurice Abravanel came in 1951 and stayed for 25 years. Noted baritone Martial Singher joined the faculty in 1950, succeeding Lehmann as voice director in 1962. He stayed until he died, actually living at Miraflores toward the end. All three of these people shaped the Music Academy into one of the finest summer institutes, rivaling the best in Europe and elsewhere. Their legacies are noted throughout the community, as their names grace concert halls and studios at Miraflores and UCSB.

HERBERT BAYER'S SCULPTURE
"Chromatic Gate," on the Santa
Barbara oceanfront, is one of
many pieces of public artwork
throughout the South Coast.

Santa Barbara Out-of-Doors

Santa Barbara's natural environment is without question the reason it came to be called Paradise on the Pacific.

Temperatures throughout the year average about 70 degrees. Although morning fog is common in June, it keeps the area from becoming overly hot. Yet warm and sunny Christmases are common.

*S*anta Barbara's climate is so idyllic largely because of the area's south-facing beaches, which bring warm ocean breezes ashore, and the transversal Santa Ynez mountain range, which protects the South Coast from northern winter storms. There are only four other ranges in the world that run east to west as the range does here. In addition to the obvious climatic advantages, the east-west alignment makes the South Coast—and Cachuma Lake just over the range—a stopping-off point for hundreds of species of migratory birds.

CHANNEL ISLANDS

Contributing to the South Coast's famous Mediterranean climate are the Channel Islands off the coast, which protect the region from fierce storms coming off the ocean. There are eight islands in the Channel Islands chain, of which four are less than 30 miles from Santa Barbara. The largest island, Santa Cruz, about 26 miles from shore, is also the closest. Nearby are Santa Rosa, San Miguel, and Anacapa. The more remote islands—southeast of the South Coast—are Santa Barbara, San Nicolas, and San Clemente. Santa Catalina, off Los Angeles, is also part of the Channel Islands chain.

On clear days one can see all four of the islands immediately off Santa Barbara, and they are resplendent. San Miguel is the most westerly, followed by Santa Rosa, Santa Cruz, and Anacapa. These four—plus Santa Barbara Island—are now a national park and marine sanctuary. One, Santa Cruz Island, is largely owned by the Nature Conservancy. A small portion of Santa Cruz's eastern end, about 10 percent, is still in private hands. It is expected to be purchased by the federal government and added to the park by the end of the century. An agreement with the previous owners of Santa Rosa Island allows a decades-old cattle ranch to continue operations there, although the island is now owned by the government.

Channel Islands National Park is undoubtedly one of the least visited national parks—for a couple of reasons, the most obvious of which is that it isn't particularly easy to get there. Commercial boat excursions to the islands operate mostly out of Ventura, 30 miles south of Santa Barbara. And some or most portions of each island are off-limits during all or part of the year because they contain rare or endangered species. To visit Santa Cruz Island, one must get permission from the private property owners or the Nature Conservancy, which limits access but helps preserve the island's sensitive ecosystem.

Nonetheless, a trip to one or more of the Channel Islands can be an experience of a lifetime. Anacapa Island is considered one of the finest diving spots in the world. Dive boats operate year-round out of Sea Landing harbor in Santa Barbara. Huge flowing underwater kelp forests are home to a vast variety of colorful sea creatures that swim midstream rather than at the bottom, as in many tropical areas, making viewing easier. A portion of west Anacapa Island is closed from January 1 through October 31, the nesting season of the brown pelican.

All of the islands have colonies of seals, walruses, or other pinnipeds. San Miguel, the most barren of the islands, is home to six species of pinnipeds, including a large rookery of elephant seals, harbor seals, sea lions, and the endangered Guadalupe fur seal. San Miguel also has the only breeding colony of northern fur seals south of the Pribilof Islands off Alaska.

Visitors to San Miguel must be accompanied by a ranger beyond the beach at Cuyler Harbor. Day hikes from Cuyler Harbor to Point Bennett to see the elephant seal rookery can be arranged through the U.S. Park Service. The trek is about 15 miles round trip.

Santa Barbara Island is the most remote of the park islands. Considered most like a sea island, it has steep cliffs and a large assortment of birds and marine wildlife.

Generally, day and overnight trips to Santa Barbara, Santa Rosa, Anacapa, and San Miguel Islands can be handled through Island Packers in Ventura or Sea Landing in Santa Barbara. The Santa Barbara Museum of Natural History also sponsors tours to the islands each year. It takes some planning to visit one or more of them, but they offer some of the most spectacular scenery and wildlife and a bit of California history untold anywhere else.

On clear days, the islands appear to be little more than a footstep from Santa Barbara. They add to the image of sea, sun, and sand that so many people associate with the region.

Kid's World features a fierce-looking land-locked shark and a friendly whale for climbing. Across town, volleyball is a longtime staple at East Beach, where nets are maintained year-round.

SUN, SAND, AND FUN

Beaches certainly are a major part of life in Santa Barbara. A good portion of the coastline through the city is in public hands. East Beach, where volleyball champ Karch Kiraly trained as a UCSB student, anchors a continuous stretch of shoreline for several miles. It includes Chase Palm Park, the foot of Stearns Wharf, West Beach, the harbor, Leadbetter Beach, and, finally, Shoreline Park. The city's main thoroughfare, State Street, runs straight through downtown to Stearns Wharf, constantly beckoning to the beach and ocean. Sculptor Bud Bottoms's famous dolphin fountain anchors the wharf at Cabrillo Boulevard and has become one of the most recognizable Santa Barbara icons.

Cabrillo Boulevard, which parallels the oceanfront, is a focal point for residents and visitors alike. Hotels and restaurants line the mountain side. Parks dominate the ocean side.

Fess Parker's Red Lion Resort and the Santa Barbara Radisson are two of the more famous lodgings along the boulevard. The Red Lion has the distinction of having been built in the 1980s with the specific imprimatur of Santa Barbara's voters, who approved it overwhelmingly. One of Santa Barbara's more unusual pieces of public art, sculptor Herbert Bayer's "Chromatic Gate," stands dramatically in front of the Red Lion on a small plot of green parkway.

Interspersed with these well-known hostelries are smaller hotels and motels, restaurants, and funky burger joints. A public beachway that runs the length of Cabrillo Boulevard allows bicyclists, four-wheel surrey riders, and roller-bladers recreational passage. Pedestrians also are allowed, but common sense advises to stay to the grassy areas and away from the freewheeling fun-seekers. They can be daunting to a stroller.

Across the street from the Radisson is the Cabrillo Pavilion Arts Center. It once served as one of two bathhouses at the beach. The other bathhouse, at West Beach next to Santa Barbara Harbor, is Los Banos del Mar—the bath by the sea. Recently renovated, this historic community swimming pool now has a new liner, a deck, and access for the disabled, as well as new locker rooms. Los Banos del Mar is one of two community pools (the other is Ortega Park Pool) operated by the Santa Barbara Parks and Recreation Department.

Parks and Recreation offers a wide variety of activities for children and teens, including summertime and after-school recreation programs, dances, theater and ballet classes, arts and crafts programs, and a wide assortment of sports activities. The department also offers swimming, dance, music, art, and fitness programs for adults and services and classes for seniors.

The city has dozens of parks, and most are available for group rental. One of the more popular parks for weddings and other big events is Las Positas Friendship Park, which has spectacular views of the ocean from its hilltop amphitheater and grove. Other favorite spots are Shoreline Park, Alameda Park, and Alice Keck Park Memorial Gardens downtown.

Youngsters especially enjoy Alameda Park—home to Kid's World. One of the most used—and beautiful—playgrounds in the city, Kid's World came about through the efforts of 4,000 children and their parents, who helped design and then construct this wonderful 7,000-square-foot playground. Today, Kid's World features mazes, castlelike turrets and bridges, tunnels and slides,

SAILING IS A FAVORITE
pastime on the South Coast,
where gentle breezes and the mild
climate make ocean-going easy
and enjoyable.

A VOLLEYBALL EXHIBITION FEATURES
national champ Karch Kiraly, who
attended the University of California
at Santa Barbara and honed his skills
here at East Beach.

swings and monkey bars, a tot yard, balancing beams, and a life-size whale and shark to climb on.

Another park favored by locals is Arroyo Burro, at the end of Cliff Drive just west of its intersection with Las Positas Road. It is commonly called Hendry's beach, after the family that once owned the land. Arroyo Burro is often mistaken as a city park but actually is part of the county park system. Arroyo Burro is the place to explore tide pools, climb rocks, and watch hang-gliders descend from the hilltops just above. Dolphins and sea lions are common sights off shore, as are whales during whale-watching season. The beach tends to be less breezy and perhaps even a little warmer than the beaches along Cabrillo Boulevard.

Other county parks in the Goleta area include Goleta Beach, Lake Los Carneros, Stow Grove, and San Antonio Canyon (also called Tucker's Grove). Manning Park in Montecito is a shady expanse of lawn that makes a wonderful picnic spot, while Rocky Nook Park near the Santa Barbara Mission features a gurgling (sometimes rumbling) Mission Creek. Most county parks feature playground equipment and picnic facilities. Two parks, Arroyo Burro and Goleta Beach, not only have snack bars but fine restaurants on site.

ZOOLOGICAL GARDENS

In addition to parks, the South Coast is home to one of the world's finest small zoos, the Santa Barbara Zoological Gardens, and two fabulous botanic gardens: Lotusland and the Santa Barbara Botanic Garden in Mission Canyon.

The zoo is at 500 Ninos Lane, just off Cabrillo Boulevard and across from East Beach. The 81-acre property was originally part of a palatial estate owned by Lillian Child, and one can still see portions of the foundation of the old estate house at the top of the hill. Child donated the land to the city in 1951, and in 1962 the Child Estate Foundation was organized to create a park. In 1963, the zoo was opened to the public.

The American Association of Zoological Parks and Aquariums has recognized the Zoological Gardens as a model of excellence among small zoos. It has more than 600 animals (and 150 species) in state-of-the-art enclosures designed to closely resemble their natural habitats.

The zoo is active in a national breeding effort to save rare and endangered animals. Some of its more notable creatures are a brother-sister pair of African lions, rare Baringo giraffes, California sea lions, two Asian elephants, a large flock of Chilean flamingos, ruffed and ring-tailed lemurs, white-handed gibbons, and a wide assortment of birds, reptiles, and other creatures. The zoo's newest exhibit will house the endangered mountain gorilla of Rwanda. Also featured are a miniature train ride, a carousel, and a playground, as well as picnic grounds, a snack bar, and a gift shop.

BOTANIC GARDENS

Lotusland is one of the South Coast's most beautiful and exclusive garden estates. Once the pride and joy of Madame Ganna Walska, an eccentric opera singer, it is now owned by a nonprofit organization dedicated to preserving and enhancing the gardens through educational tours.

Lotusland features rare and unusual plants from around the world, including a large collection of cycads, which look much like palms but are actually more closely related to pine trees. Lotusland also features a spectacular Japanese garden; the Blue Garden, featuring specimens with blue foliage; and the incredible Water Gardens, whose vast collection of lotus plants lent the estate its name.

Tours of Lotusland are given twice a day Wednesdays through Saturdays from mid-February through mid-November. Reservations are required far in advance since space is limited, but the two-hour tour is worth the wait.

Less unusual but equally beautiful is the Santa Barbara Botanic Garden, which has an extensive collection of vegetation native to California, including trees, wild flowers, and cacti. Nearly six miles of trails wind through the 65-acre garden, which is divided into sections to showcase the various flora. California meadows, deserts, manzanita, woodland, canyon, and island areas are represented. A portion of the trail crosses a century-old dam built by Chumash Indians to provide water to the old Santa Barbara Mission. The Botanic Garden is at 1212 Mission Canyon Road, in the foothills overlooking the Santa Barbara Mission.

AGAVE IS ONE OF THOUSANDS of plant varieties that visitors admire at the Santa Barbara Botanic Garden, in Mission Canyon.

LAKE CACHUMA

ust 40 miles north of Santa Barbara on scenic Highway 154 are Cachuma Lake and the county's Cachuma Lake Recreation Area. Built in the 1950s, the lake is the source of most of the drinking water in the South Coast and portions of the Santa Ynez Valley. As important, though, the lake has become a crucial habitat for a great diversity of wildlife, including four pairs of nesting American bald eagles.

Because of the lake's role as a provider of fresh drinking water, no swimming, wading, or water skiing is allowed. But the recreation area offers wonderful lakeside camping, hiking, boating, fishing, and many other outdoor activities. There are campsites for tents and hookups for recreational vehicles. A general store has every forgotten necessity, and a large public pool is available for swimming.

But to many, the most enjoyable and educational activities offered at the lake are the boat tours, which

Lake Cachuma boat tours with park naturalist Neal Taylor offer a glimpse of the wildlife that live in and around this man-made lake.

enable visitors to observe the bald eagles and other wildlife up close. The park's naturalist, Neal Taylor, is extremely knowledgeable about the animals, trees and plant life, and geologic development of the region. A boat tour with Taylor, who gave up a corporate job to become a naturalist, is both informative and entertaining.

Cachuma Lake has 32 miles of shoreline. Most of the northern shore is in Los Padres National Forest and is thus protected from human encroachment. Bald eagles nested in the region before the lake was filled in the late 1950s and didn't return until 1981. That year, a nesting pair was spied at the same 9-foot-wide, 23-foot-deep nest that had been abandoned all those years earlier.

Today, many other eagles stop over at the lake to join the nesting pairs, and park officials hope that eventually more will take up residence. Bald eagles are truly incredible birds to see, and boat tours almost always catch sight of at least one, either on the wing or perched in a tall snag near the shoreline.

The eagle boat tours are offered from November through March, when the eagles are most likely to be seen around the lake. The rest of the year, the tours focus on the wildlife that live near Cachuma, including mountain lions and bobcats, mule deer, endangered pond turtles, and hundreds of species of birds, such as kingfishers, herons, osprey, and golden eagles.

Hundreds of years ago, the region was home to a thriving Chumash culture, and thousands of artifacts have been found here. The area was home to seven Chumash villages and 32 native sites. Construction of the reservoir would never be allowed today because of the historical significance of the area. This is all the more reason, in Taylor's view, to expose as many people as possible to what was here and to the value of the natural environment that nurtures such a rich assortment of wildlife today.

A peek at Lake Cachuma in the Santa Ynez Valley, from the ruins of an old ranch homestead

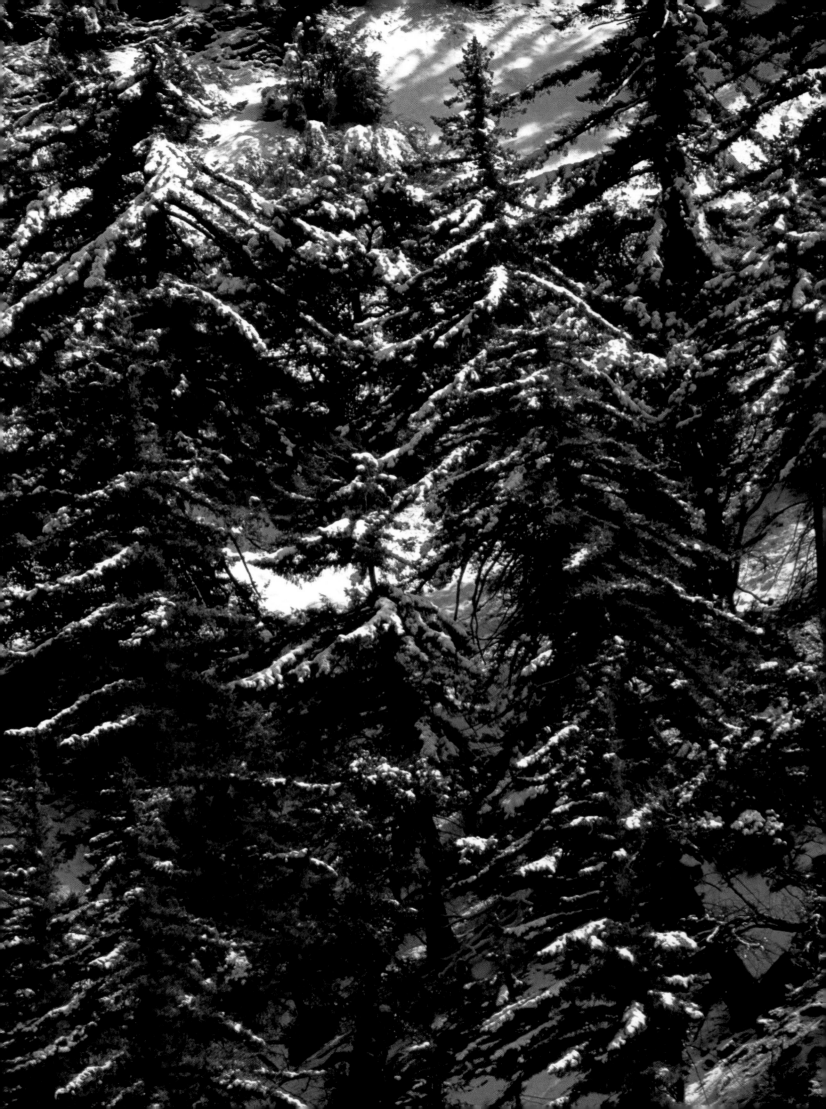

One tree that isn't native to California—the Australian eucalyptus—is responsible for one of the more magnificent sights along the coast every fall. Eucalyptus groves have become a favored wintering ground for migrating monarch butterflies. At times, the orange-and-black insects are so thick in the trees that they appear to be ablaze. When chill begins to grip the inland California valleys, monarchs seek the relatively frost-free conditions of the coast. Plenty of milkweed and the eucalyptus trees combine to create an excellent mating ground for the butterflies. Some come from as far away as Nevada. They winter at spots from Monterey to Ensenada, Mexico. In Santa Barbara County, they are often most abundant in Ellwood, at the far western reaches of Goleta Valley; at the nearby Dos Pueblos Ranch; and at the Music Academy of the West, in Montecito.

Migrating creatures greatly enrich Santa Barbara County. Residents have come to eagerly anticipate the arrival of California gray whales as they make their way south in the fall and north in the springtime and the return of the bald eagles at Cachuma Lake every fall.

Though Cachuma Lake Recreation Area is a county park, it is situated in the middle of Los Padres National Forest, which provides year-round recreational activities ranging from fishing, hiking, and camping to more rigorous adventures into the backcountry wilderness.

The national forest also includes a good portion of the foothills of Santa Barbara. Dozens of hiking trails go up the various canyons along stream beds that, if the area has a wet winter, can rage with springtime runoff.

The Santa Ynez Mountains rise up from the ocean, ranging generally from 3,000 to 5,000 feet in elevation. Behind the Santa Ynez Mountains is the San Rafael range, gateway to the Dick Smith and San Rafael wilderness areas. The tallest peak in the national forest is Big Pine Mountain, at 6,828 feet. In winter, it's not unusual to see a dusting of snow across the mountaintops.

Few roads lead into the Los Padres National Forest, and those that do are often unpaved, narrow, and winding. There are several campgrounds, although most offer only rudimentary amenities: fire pits, picnic tables, and outhouse-type restrooms. Still, for many visitors, the solitude and wildlife are more than worth the effort of getting there.

Entering the backcountry is even more challenging. Backpacking and equestrian camping, which require permits, are popular activities in the wilderness areas. But, as some visitors discover, the mountains also hold treasures.

This remote region has some of the finest examples of Chumash rock art, dating back hundreds, perhaps thousands, of years. The Chumash lived throughout the central California coast area and on the Channel Islands. Their pictographs have been found at sites throughout the region, but none are so colorful and elaborate as those found in the deep mountains. All have been discovered near permanent water sites and range from drawings on the interiors of hidden caves to adornments along cliff edges and on towering rocks. Most are in red, black, and white, though some of the more complex paintings incorporate yellow and pale green.

The images are fanciful from a modern point of view. Many reflect what appear to be marine or aquatic animals. Some defy understanding. There are sun shapes and brightly colored geometric designs. There are human forms; one drawing depicts horsemen. Scientists believe the various designs had religious significance, but that is something we will never know for sure. The site of the most famous of the Chumash rock paintings, located at the top of the Santa Ynez Mountains, is known today as Painted Cave. Discovered in the early 1900s, the area is now a state historical park, where visitors can view the images on the cave walls through a locked grill gate.

Scientists have worked over the past few decades to preserve what are left of the original Chumash pictographs and to document ones they cannot save. A recent find in a San Nicolas Island cave has excited the scientific world. Its entrance is a small crevice at the tide line on the south side of the island. The Cave of the Whales, as researchers call it, is 135 feet deep and has towering walls and ceiling. The entrance is marked by a boulder featuring a three-foot-long pictograph of a marine animal. Concerned that some of the pictographs are being worn away by the environment, scientists from the Santa Barbara Museum of Natural History are leading an effort to document the cave's interior, so that future generations can appreciate what has been called some of the finest Native American art.

THE NATIONAL HORSE SHOW,
held each year at the Earl Warren
Showgrounds, draws champions from
across the country. At right, visitors
and residents alike enjoy sidewalk dining at cafes up and down State Street
in downtown Santa Barbara.

THE SANTA BARBARA CHANNEL
is one of the few places where
magnificent blue whales are
consistently sighted during
migrations. Whale watching has
become one of the South Coast's
biggest seasonal businesses.

A SOLITARY HERON SITS
on Arroyo Burro Beach
at low tide. The beach,
nicknamed Hendry's, is
a favorite with locals.

LEFT, A CATAMARAN SKIMS ALONG
off the Santa Barbara coastline.
Above, a hang-glider launches
from East Camino Cielo, far
above the city, to drift lazily
down on the warm air currents
that blow off the ocean.

FIVE

Excellence in Education, for Children and Adults

E ducational opportunities are abundant in Santa Barbara, from preschools to graduate-level institutions. A strong emphasis on learning and support for both public and private schools contribute to an atmosphere conducive to lifelong education.

ELEMENTARY AND SECONDARY SCHOOLS

The South Coast's elementary and secondary public school system is very good. The area is also privileged to have a wide variety of excellent private schools.

In Carpinteria, where less-expensive housing is an attractive draw for Santa Barbara professionals, the Carpinteria Unified School District offers an early childhood learning center, four elementary schools, a middle school, and Carpinteria High School.

Montecito has two public school districts, each with one elementary school: Montecito Union and Cold Spring. Both are considered among the finest elementary schools in the region.

In Santa Barbara, there are two public school districts, but they share the same school board and administration. The elementary district has 10 schools within the city of Santa Barbara. Two—Peabody Charter and the Open Alternative School—offer alternative curriculums and staffing structures. The broader high school district has three high schools and four junior highs that serve the Santa Barbara city elementary schools as well as those of Montecito, Goleta Union, and Hope School Districts.

Hope School District serves a portion of the community that lies roughly around the western boundary of the city and the Goleta Valley. It has two schools—Monte Vista and Vieja Valley—and in 1995, it announced it would open a third campus to accommodate growth in student population. The Hope District schools also enjoy a reputation in the community for providing exceptional education.

Like Hope, the Goleta Union School District has been experiencing student growth in recent years and is making changes in its facilities to accommodate the increase. The district operates eight elementary schools and an early childhood education center.

There are a large number of private elementary and secondary schools to choose from, ranging from traditional parochial schools run by religious congregations to nondenominational schools that offer specialized curriculums and college preparatory instruction.

For students at the elementary level, there is the Howard School in Montecito, which emphasizes the Carden curriculum, based on the philosophy of Mae Carden, who taught that children want to learn and thus should enjoy learning.

Programs at the school, which was founded in 1912 and is the oldest private elementary school in the Santa Barbara area, are structured to reinforce positive messages, and children are taught to think independently and creatively. Classical literature, poetry, language arts, mathematics, geography, history, science, sports, and the arts are emphasized, as is an appreciation of nature.

Also in Montecito is the Crane School, founded as a boys school by William D. Crane in 1928. Within a few years it became co-educational. Crane was established with what would today be called progressive educational principles. It has a rigorous academic curriculum and emphasizes learning by doing. Its reputation for innovation remains strong today. Crane serves 212 students from kindergarten through eighth grade.

There are three Montessori schools on the South Coast: Montessori Center School and Montessori Santa Barbara School in Santa Barbara and Montessori Sunrise School in Montecito. They all follow the Montessori curriculum, which emphasizes independent, self-directed learning.

The Waldorf School in Santa Barbara offers a progressive, art-centered curriculum for kindergartners through eighth-graders. Located on the grounds of the former St. Anthony's Seminary near the Santa Barbara Mission, Waldorf emphasizes the use of imagination, play, creativity, and intuition, in the belief that children learn through ways other than the strictly intellectual.

Sharing St. Anthony's campus is Santa Barbara Middle School, for sixth through ninth graders. Established in 1976, the school serves about 140 students. The curriculum is multidimensional but emphasizes outdoor education. Students and staff go on backpacking and bike trips throughout the academic year. The other three areas of focus are academics, community service, and the creative arts.

Laguna Blanca School was founded in 1933 on 27 acres in the affluent Hope Ranch area of Santa Barbara. The school offers classes from kindergarten through 12th grades and emphasizes individual development in both academics and athletics. A particular focus is placed on public speaking and awareness of current events. The school also expects students to provide service to their community.

McKinley Elementary School is one of many high-quality schools in Santa Barbara. Many of the older schools in the city reflect the Mediterranean architectural style.

SANTA BARBARA JUNIOR HIGH
School is one of the city's most
beautiful and historic structures,
not to mention an important
learning environment for the
community's adolescents.

BABATUNDE FOLAYEMI—
A FRIEND TO KIDS

Some kids in Santa Barbara would literally be lost without Babatunde Folayemi. Programs director for the Santa Barbara Housing Authority, Folayemi has developed and won grants for his innovative youth programs, which have helped untold numbers of teens not only succeed in high school but go on to college. And, in the process, they have stayed clear of gangs and potentially trouble with the criminal justice system. Most of these youngsters live on the city's lower Eastside and Westside, where many economically disadvantaged families live.

Folayemi's efforts have resulted in many wonderful programs, including the Ortega Park Summer Program, which provides basketball, soccer, and other recreational activities for Santa Barbara's

youth. One of his newest efforts is Tribe, a cultural, educational, recreational, and leadership training program. Nearly 50 youngsters are regular participants, and more than 150 are signed up. Daily tutoring and individual classes in ethnic studies, computer technology, crafts, and leadership training are offered.

Coming soon is Street Law, intended to bring local jurists and attorneys together with teens so they can gain a clearer understanding of the law as it applies to them.

Folayemi and his wife moved to Santa Barbara from Malibu in the mid-1980s. The owner of a company that manufactured activewear, Folayemi commuted for two years before selling his company and settling into a position as projects coordinator with a non-profit group called the Alliance for Community Development. When the organization folded in the early 1990s, the Housing Authority hired Folayemi to continue his work in developing youth programs.

Folayemi started working with youngsters in Harlem in the 1960s during what he calls the "old antipoverty [program] days." He also spent a lot of time with youth in Los Angeles during his years in that city, all the while developing his business interests and raising a son.

Folayemi sees tremendous need among our youngsters, but also tremendous hope. With the recent trend toward cutbacks in government funding, he believes the private sector is an untapped resource for kids and is working to develop job-training programs with Santa Barbara businesses.

One of the most innovative projects Folayemi is developing involves a partnership with the Santa Barbara Museum of Natural History. Through work-training programs, youngsters will be exposed to unusual fields, such as marine biology and vertebrate and invertebrate studies.

"Santa Barbara's people are really willing to help," Folayemi says. "Santa Barbara is small enough where you can really make a difference."

Babatunde Folayemi certainly has, and because of him, the community's youngsters—indeed all of Santa Barbara—have benefited tremendously.

There are several private schools that provide intensive college preparatory instruction for junior and senior high school students.

The Anacapa School, founded in 1981 in downtown Santa Barbara, prides itself on providing personalized education. The curriculum emphasizes college preparation through academic study, social and personal development, and the acquisition of critical thinking skills. Citizenship and the development of knowledge and understanding of the world at large are emphasized as well.

The prestigious Cate School was founded by Curtis Wolsey Cate and his brother, Karl, in 1910. Hailed today as one of the finest college-prep schools in the country, the school started out in a house in Mission Canyon with 12 boys. The Cates called the school the Miramar School, then changed it to the Santa Barbara School the following year, when Curtis Cate moved the campus to a ranch in Carpinteria. A few years later the campus was moved to its current mesa location in Carpinteria. When Cate retired as headmaster in 1950, the school was renamed in his honor.

Cate remained a boys school until 1981. Today, girls make up just under 50 percent of the student body. Students come from all over the world and pay the equivalent of an Ivy League college tuition. (In the 1995–96 school year, it was $20,600 for a boarding student.) But a Cate education is considered worth the cost. In 1987, Harvard's *Insider's Guide to Prep Schools* ranked Cate one of the nation's top 10 independent prep schools. It was the only school listed that was outside New England.

SANTA BARBARA CITY COLLEGE

Santa Barbara City College is considered one of the finest community colleges in the state. Housed on a campus perched on a mesa overlooking the ocean, it certainly is the most picturesque. Sweeping vistas of the shoreline and harbor make studying here a privilege.

But the college has much more to offer than just a beautiful campus. It also has a rich and varied curriculum, suited both to students who plan to go on to universities and to adults looking to take courses for vocational or personal enrichment. City College's Continuing Education Division is the largest in the state and has won praise as one of the most innovative in the nation.

City College was founded in 1909 by the Santa Barbara High School District. The school was disbanded after World War I, then reestablished in 1946 to serve returning servicemen. Today, the college serves more than 10,000 students enrolled in day and evening classes, while adult education classes attract another 37,000 each year.

The college offers transfer programs for students who wish to continue their studies at a university. The college also offers associate degree and certificate programs in a wide variety of occupational fields. Academic and personal counseling, career guidance, and financial assistance programs also are available.

The college recently embarked on an assessment of its entire curriculum and how it packages courses. Under development are new programs that will take advantage of the latest in computer technology.

PRIVATE COLLEGES AND INSTITUTES

The South Coast also is home to a host of private undergraduate and graduate-level schools and institutes.

Westmont College in Montecito is a small liberal arts institution that emphasizes a Christian-based philosophy. Students must live on campus for at least the first two years of study, and extensive community service is required for graduation. Westmont students contribute both their time and energy to dozens of local charities and are well known among parents for being some of the best baby sitters around. They often help elderly neighbors trim hedges or fix up houses. During spring break, a contingent of students travels to Mexico to build medical clinics and provide other services in poor rural villages.

Westmont was founded in Los Angeles in 1940 but was relocated to Montecito in 1945. Today, Westmont has 1,200 students, 85 percent of whom live on campus. The college prefers to maintain a residential environment, believing it is part of its unique Christian educational experience. Recognizing that it is sometimes difficult to retain good instructors in a community where housing is expensive, the school is in the process of building a 41-unit faculty housing complex next to the campus.

The western campus of Santa Barbara City College, one of the finest community colleges in California, is the latest addition to the seaside school.

For adults who work full time but want to pursue a degree or change careers or directions, there is Antioch University. An extension of the university based in Ohio, Santa Barbara's campus celebrates its 20th anniversary in 1996. Among Antioch's offerings are bachelor's degree programs in communications, business management, psychology, and health services management and master's degree programs in organizational management and clinical psychology.

In 1995, Antioch had about 260 students, representing a 60 percent increase since 1988. In coming years Antioch hopes to purchase a permanent site near its currently leased quarters in downtown Santa Barbara, which would enable it to expand its enrollment to about 450 students.

Like Antioch, the private Fielding Institute in Santa Barbara and the Pacifica Graduate Institute in Carpinteria offer graduate-level courses in psychology.

Another private educational institute with a national reputation is the Brooks Institute of Photography & Filmmaking. Founded in 1945 by Ernest Brooks Sr.,

the institute offers bachelor's degrees in several disciplines involving still photography and motion picture production. It also offers a master of science degree in photography, as well as extension courses.

Brooks has three campuses: at the breathtaking Graholm estate in Montecito; the Jefferson campus, on what is known as the Riviera in Santa Barbara (with a stunning view of the city and ocean); and in downtown Santa Barbara. The downtown campus houses the School of Motion Picture, which has the most extensive undergraduate filmmaking curriculum in the world.

Santa Barbara also has its own law school, the Southern California Institute of Law.

UCSB

Without a doubt, UCSB is the sparkling gem of educational offerings on the South Coast. The campus celebrated its 50th anniversary in 1995, making it a veritable babe in university terms. But, in spite of its youth, in 1994, it was ranked one of the nation's top research universities

The Engineering Building is one of several new structures at UCSB. Right, UCSB's landmark Storke Tower, named for the publisher of the Santa Barbara News-Press *who helped persuade the California legislature to establish the campus.*

by the Carnegie Commission, 39th among 88 "Research I" universities and 21st among public "Research I" schools. To be defined as a Research I university, a school has to graduate at least 50 doctoral students and have garnered more than $40 million in federal grants during a two-year period. In fact, in 1994 alone, UCSB received $81 million in federal, state, and private research funds.

In 1995, the campus was admitted to the prestigious Association of American Universities and was ranked by *Science Watch*, an Institute for Scientific Information publication, as among the nation's top 10 research universities. Also in 1995, the National Research Council ranked 10 UCSB graduate programs as among the nation's best. Among 3,600 doctoral programs in 41 fields, UCSB's geography program ranked fourth in the nation; materials science, eighth; religious studies, ninth; and physics, 10th. In addition, UCSB's graduate programs in chemical engi-

neering, anthropology, Spanish, electrical engineering, biology-ecology, and geosciences were ranked among the top 20 in the nation.

The college had humble beginnings as a teachers college. It later became Santa Barbara State College. In the early 1950s, Thomas M. Storke, publisher of the *Santa Barbara News-Press*, and civic leader Pearl Chase launched a major campaign aimed at making the college part of the University of California (UC) system.

With two liberal arts campuses already in the system—UC Berkeley and UC Los Angeles—the board of regents was reluctant to add Santa Barbara. Storke and Chase persisted, and the board finally relented. But, as professors remember, the system paid little attention to UCSB at first. In fact, professors were paid less than other UC faculty, and the school was limited to undergraduate education.

A GUIDING LIGHT
IN ADULT EDUCATION

Santa Barbara City College's Continuing Education Division is one of the nation's finest, and most of its success is due to Selmer O. "Sam" Wake. Wake was named director of the community's adult education program in 1947 and guided it through the early 1970s, creating one of the most innovative and widely used curriculums in the country.

Today, more than 37,000 Santa Barbarans—nearly one in four residents—take adult education courses each year. Clearly, the reason is the diversity of choices and the high caliber of the speakers and instructors.

Santa Barbara's adult education program offers more than 2,400 courses each year—from the creative arts to current affairs, health instruction to personal development, parent education to vocational training. In fact, the program has more classes registered with the state office of education than California's two largest community college adult ed programs combined.

Sam Wake is the reason.

Wake came to Santa Barbara in 1939 at the urging of a colleague at the University of Oregon, where he had earned bachelor's and master's degrees in industrial engineering and education. He taught here for seven years, then accepted a position as apprenticeship coordinator and counselor in adult education. A year later he was appointed director. At the time, the program was growing. Returning GIs flocked to the classes, as did defense workers seeking civilian employment skills.

But Wake saw a need to provide more than vocational instruction and what is typically considered adult ed fare. He began to offer current events discussions, wading into such controversial topics as nuclear war, communism, and the Red Scare in the McCarthy years; the value of the U.S. Constitution when the John Birch Society flourished; a series on religion and faith; and heated community issues.

The topics alone drew crowds, but Wake also brought in famous speakers and panelists, including Senator Eugene McCarthy, Norman Cousins, and William Saroyan. Wake's legacy is that the program continues to bring some of the nation's most interesting and learned people to the community to contribute to adult ed classes.

Wake "retired" in 1972 but immediately took on the task of forming and developing a foundation for Santa Barbara City College. Seven years later, when the foundation surpassed its first million-dollar mark, Wake "retired" again. Today, he is still active with several committees of the Santa Barbara Citizens' Continuing Education Advisory Council, a group of 40 community members who help guide the program through feedback and curriculum development.

Brooks photography students take aim at the old mission.

The Concours d'Elegance fund-raiser at the stunning Santa Barbara City College campus draws crowds each year.

In 1954, an old Marine Corps base at Goleta Point was purchased, and the campus moved to the 400-acre ocean-front property where it now sits. It is one of the few university campuses located on the Pacific Ocean, leading to the natural development of top-rated marine science programs.

UCSB started to bloom in the 1960s. Chancellor Vernon Cheadle, whose name graces the administration building on campus, led a period of growth that included construction of 25 new buildings and the hiring of hundreds of new faculty members. By the time Cheadle retired in 1977, UCSB had become a recognized research institution with more than 14,000 students and 42 master's degree and 27 doctorate programs.

Among many milestones that occurred in the years that followed were the creation of the Institute of Theoretical Physics (ITP). When the institute was proposed by four UCSB professors in 1979, their idea was to create a dynamic, interactive institute where international researchers could come to collaborate on interdisciplinary

subjects with postdoctoral students. After five years of operation, the National Science Foundation gave the institute permanent standing.

Today, the ITP sponsors four six-month programs a year, on subjects such as planet formation, high-temperature superconductors, string theory, quasicrystals, solar seismology, cosmology and microphysics, and quantum chromodynamics.

Another National Science Foundation–supported institute at UCSB is the Center for the Study of Quantized Electronic Structures (QUEST). Researchers here are at the forefront of efforts to develop new materials that will allow for further miniaturization of electronic circuitry. These so-called quantum-effect electronics materials are being used by UCSB's Opto-electronics Technology Center to further develop advanced devices such as semiconductor lasers and optical modulators.

UCSB's College of Engineering is also at the forefront of research in advanced materials. Scientists are working on condensed matter physics, polymer science, and

Graduation ceremonies at UCSB often occur under sunny skies amid light ocean breezes.

electronic materials. One expert, materials scientist Anthony Evans, is collaborating with Carnegie Mellon University scientists to duplicate the layered structure of natural materials using ceramics, polymers, and metals.

UCSB geographers have been at the leading edge of environmental research for more than 15 years. The first formal discussions of the global impact of human activity were held at UCSB in 1979 and 1980. Today, 40 researchers from nine departments are working on this topic. The new School of Environmental Science and Management is the first school of its kind to focus on global change.

UCSB also is home to the Institute for Crustal Studies, whose scientists are conducting pioneering research on earthquakes. The campus's geographers are considered leaders in the development of something called geographic information systems, used in navigating during deep-sea diving excursions and in studies of the effects of ozone depletion on marine life.

Santa Barbara's Marine Science Institute is also considered one of the nation's best. The devastating 1969 oil spill in the Santa Barbara Channel led to the creation of the institute. Institute scientists have been consultants on the effects and cleanup of the world's worst oil spills, including the 1989 *Exxon Valdez* spill off Alaska.

One of the most unusual and interesting discoveries of UCSB marine scientists is the existence of colonies of deep-sea creatures that rely on chemicals, rather than sunlight, for sustenance. Six-foot tubeworms, giant clams, and two dozen other species were found thriving in total darkness near volcanic vents that spewed 400-degree water laden with sulfur and other minerals near the bottom of the ocean.

Sometimes it seems much of the world-class research at UCSB goes without notice in the Santa Barbara community. But the South Coast benefits mightily from the intellectual environment that nurtures such research and from the knowledge-based businesses that are natural spin-offs of these endeavors.

*S*ANTA *B*ARBARA'S *B*USINESS *E*NVIRONMENT

S ANTA BARBARA'S ECONOMY IS BUILT ON MANY INDUSTRIES—RETAILING, TOURISM, HIGH-TECHNOLOGY MANUFACTURING, BUSINESS AND HEALTH SERVICES, AND AGRICULTURE, AMONG OTHERS. THE SOUTH COAST BOASTS MORE THAN 18,000 BUSINESSES, 85 PERCENT OF WHICH HAVE FEWER THAN 10 EMPLOYEES. THE LARGEST EMPLOYERS ARE UCSB; THE COUNTY GOVERNMENT; COTTAGE HOSPITAL; AND THE HIGH-TECH COMPANIES—E-SYSTEMS (FORMERLY RAYTHEON COMPANY), DELCO, APPLIED MAGNETICS, AND THE SANTA BARBARA RESEARCH CENTER.

Because Santa Barbarans have a strong desire to maintain their stunningly beautiful natural environment, such traditional powerhouse industries as construction and heavy manufacturing do not figure heavily in the economy. What does exist is a nurturing environment for small knowledge-based companies, incubated and fed to a large degree by the brain trust at UCSB.

EMERGING INDUSTRIES

No new industry fits so well into the Santa Barbara philosophy on business development as the computer software industry. Though still limited, it is becoming an important force in the South Coast economy and holds promise for invigorated growth.

Most of these companies are small—fewer than 100 employees—but several have enjoyed profound success.

QAD is clearly the leader in this area. The company specializes in global supply chain management through computerization. Its software enables businesses to track manufacturing, distribution, customer services, inventory, and financial applications with one system.

Started in 1979, the company has offices in six countries, including Hong Kong and the Netherlands, and customers in 66 nations. In 1994, the company purchased a 28-acre site on Ortega Hill Road in Summerland and another 34-acre parcel in Carpinteria to expand its corporate headquarters. Founded by Pamela and Karl Lopker, both graduates of UCSB, QAD has more than 600 employees and reported revenues of more than $60 million in 1994.

Softool Corporation in Goleta, another of the region's largest software companies, was founded by a former UCSB professor and his brother in 1976. Leon Presser and his brother, Abe, left in 1995 when the company was purchased by Illinois-based Platinum Technology. Softool leads the industry in the development of "change and configuration management software." It enables programmers to make changes while developing new software without fear of adverse effects. Platinum's acquisition of Softool is expected to mean expansion of the Goleta company in coming years.

MetaTools, in Carpinteria, formerly HSC Software, also has experienced high rates of growth. Founded in 1987 by John Wilczak, HSC was a consulting company in imaging and electronic publishing. Software wizard Kai Krause joined the company in 1992, and it began developing new software tools for graphic designers, production artists, animators, and businesspeople. In 1995, Wilczak and Krause renamed the company MetaTools. The firm's award-winning "Power Tools" software has sold more than 2 million copies.

Wavefront Technologies, which developed cutting-edge computer graphics and animation technology for films, went public in 1994 and merged with Silicon Graphics and Alias Research in early 1995. Now called Alias/Wavefront, the company specializes in the development of 2D and 3D graphics and animation software for application in filmmaking, television, and computer games.

Though he's no longer with Alias/Wavefront, co-founder Larry Barels is an example of the kind of entrepreneur attracted to Santa Barbara. His story is typical of many who tailored their careers to stay in the community, rather than the other way around.

A surfer at heart, Barels first came to Santa Barbara in the 1960s when his brother was studying at UCSB. He fell in love with the quality of life afforded residents and moved here in 1970. Barels went to work for the founder of Sambo's Restaurants and stayed during that chain's phenomenal growth in the early 1970s. Between 1974 and 1984, Barels worked in real estate and consulted for a company in Denver. In 1984, he met Bill Kovacs in Los Angeles and was exposed to the graphics marketplace and the potential for computerization.

Barels and Kovacs founded Wavefront in 1983 with commercial artist Mark Sylvester. After a year, they brought out their first software product. Since then, Wavefront technology has been used in such films as *Total Recall*, *Last Action Hero*, and *Beauty and the Beast*, as well as in commercials, including "Bud Bowl VI," which ran during the Super Bowl and featured beer bottles playing a football game.

Widely regarded as one of the industry's visionaries, Barels now consults with several software development

Thousands of flights and more than half a million passengers arrive and depart each year from Santa Barbara Municipal Airport.

Magellan uses UCSB's excellent mapping and geography departments as valuable resources and has hired a number of graduates.

Computer Motion also was spawned at UCSB. Yulan Wang, who was granted UCSB's first Ph.D. in robotics, and venture capitalist Robert Duggan have developed a robotic arm that assists surgeons in operating rooms. The robot is called AESOP, for Automated Endoscopic System for Optimal Positioning. Since its advent, the device has drawn interest and investments from all over the country. In 1994, the company grew from 15 to 41 employees and moved to a 13,000-square-foot building in Goleta.

Vetronix Corporation is an automotive diagnostic equipment company that, in the process of developing new diagnostic software, tripled its Santa Barbara workforce in the early 1990s.

Another industry appears to be reemerging: filmmaking. Just after the turn of the century, Santa Barbara was home to one of the largest motion picture studios, Flying A Studios, which produced 1,200 films between 1912 and 1920. The studio took up the entire block bounded by State, Mission, Chapala, and Padre Streets. Today, the film business is more likely to be conducted on the streets and beaches of Santa Barbara, or in post-production studios tucked in and around the city.

Movie making showed strong growth in Southern California in 1995, adding enough jobs to outstrip aerospace as the largest industry in the Southland. Observers hope that as activity in Hollywood grows, it will have a positive spin-off effect in Santa Barbara.

Films are often shot in and around the South Coast, the most notable in recent years being *Steal Big, Steal Little*, produced by local resident Andy Davis. As more producers, actors, and others associated with filmmaking move to the region, it is hoped Santa Barbara will become a satellite center for the industry.

Also expected to play a large role in the future is the health and medical services industry. Cottage Hospital, Goleta Valley Community Hospital, and St. Francis Medical Center are among the leaders in the health care industry. Tenet Healthcare Corporation, one of

companies, lectures at UCSB, and is working with actor Michael Douglas (a longtime Montecito resident) on a plan to build a digital film studio on the South Coast.

Other innovative companies, such as Magellan Geographix, Computer Motion, and Vetronix Corporation, are discovering entrepreneurial uses for computer technology.

Magellan was started by UCSB graduate Rick Wood, Chris Baker, and investor Bob Temkin in 1991. It provides up-to-date electronic maps to computer users all over the world and in early 1995 started to offer its services through Compuserve. At the end of 1995, more than 3,000 maps a day were being downloaded by Compuserve users.

AN OCEANSIDE PARK SOUTH
of Carpinteria serves as a
restful noontime stop for
South Coast businesspeople.

La Tolteca

Bertha Claveria greets a visitor with the sureness of a seasoned businesswoman. She offers a seat at a table at her La Tolteca "Mexicatessen," a name she chose to replace the simpler La Tolteca Cafe. At one time the cafe was a small part of a million-dollar enterprise that she and her late husband, Federico, founded in 1946: La Tolteca Tortilla Factory. The Claverias sold the factory to a national Mexican food company in 1993. But they kept the small Haley Street cafe.

Loyal customers come, as they have for decades, for the tacos, burritos, and other Mexican delectables. Bertha Claveria calls it a Mexicatessen because of the deli items on an expanded menu. She plans to expand the restaurant, too, perhaps to a building she owns across the street.

For all their years together, Bertha Claveria was the quiet half of the partnership. Her husband, whom everyone called Fred, was outgoing and generous. Over the years he came to be called the Mayor of Haley Street, because of his activism on behalf of the Eastside neighborhood. He died in 1994, at the age of 85.

Fred and Bertha built La Tolteca Tortilla Factory into a million-dollar business with hard work, innovation, and good timing.

When they came to Santa Barbara, there was no such thing as a tortilla factory here. The Mexican families of the Eastside got their handmade tortillas from women who sold them from their homes.

The Claverias opened their first factory at 432 East Haley Street. A friend helped them design and build a conveyor-belt machine that formed the tortillas and slowly cooked them before dropping them on a table, ready for packaging.

The factory's orders grew quickly, requiring that the Claverias relocate to a new, larger location just a few blocks away. They started the restaurant to use the excess tortillas they produced. In between giving birth to her two sons, Bertha ran the restaurant.

As the business expanded, Bertha and Fred began to make tortilla chips and salsa and to sell their enchiladas and burritos in markets. Fred once told an interviewer his first day's receipts were $9.47. By the 1980s, La Tolteca was making almost three-quarters of a million tortillas a week and its annual sales exceeded $1 million.

Though the tortillas are made in Los Angeles today, they continue to be marketed under the La Tolteca name, along with the chips and salsa. And though she has no direct say over production, Bertha Claveria keeps a close eye on the quality, to ensure that they live up to the name.

A PHYSICIAN REVIEWS
X-rays at a Santa Barbara
Medical Foundation clinic.

the nation's largest hospital operators, moved its head-quarters to Santa Barbara in early 1996, bringing 90 high-wage jobs with it.

ENTREPRENEURIALISM

Some of the area's most successful companies, ones that have gone on to gain national and international recognition, grew from an entrepreneurial spirit sparked by a desire to live on the South Coast.

Sambo's Restaurants, Motel 6, and Kinko's were born and nurtured in Santa Barbara. The Territory Ahead, an international mail-order clothing company, was started by a Santa Barbara couple in 1989. Bruce Willard and Jodie Ireland began by sending out 125,000 catalogs. They did $200,000 in sales that year. In 1995, the Territory Ahead mailed more than 12 million catalogs all over the world and net revenues were expected to be $25 million.

Jandd Mountaineering, which markets backpacks and other outdoor equipment worldwide, was launched in the bathroom of an Isla Vista apartment by Dave Sisson, then a UCSB student. Deckers Outdoor Corporation in Carpinteria, which makes Teva sport sandals and the Simple shoe line, was started by QAD's Karl Lopker and two friends after they graduated from college. The company continues to have strong growth. In 1995, Deckers purchased the manufacturer of UGG boots, a trendy, sheepskin-lined boot popular with skiers and surfers.

Santa Barbara Olive Company, La Tolteca Tortilla Factory, Santa Barbara Salsa, and a host of other successful homegrown businesses have emerged from the same entrepreneurial spirit.

La Tolteca Tortilla Factory was sold to an international company several years ago, but co-founder Bertha Claveria still operates La Tolteca cafe on Haley Street, much to her customers' delight.

RETAILING

Although retailing suffered during the statewide recession of the early 1990s, signs of a turnaround were apparent by late 1995, brightening the holidays and encouraging those in the retail business. Several other factors bode well for retail as well as other businesses.

Progress was made on plans for the city to develop a large aquarium and museum complex near the waterfront, as well as to reconstruct several older buildings in the area. At the same time, the city council approved a long-range master plan for the harbor. The plan calls for a $12.5 million renovation of the waterfront over the next 10 years, which will include the construction of new boat slips at the marina and of additional public parking areas and the conversion of the historic Naval Reserve Center into a maritime museum, restaurants, and retail shops.

Discussion of one and possibly two new regional shopping centers in the Goleta Valley also encouraged those watching Santa Barbara's economy. Construction is a ways off, but observers believe at least one shopping center may be under way by the turn of the century.

With the opening of Borders Books and Music in December 1995, the community gained its eighth bookstore in the downtown corridor, adding to the nearly 60 bookstores in the county. Publishing and book retailing have always been a large presence in Santa Barbara.

There are 45 publishers in Santa Barbara County, including some large houses. One of the largest, ABC-Clio, in Goleta, specializes in technical publications. Capra Press and Daniel and Daniel concentrate on publishing local authors and books on local subjects, while McNally & Loftin focuses on books on travel, hiking, and outdoor activities. Other major houses include Harbor House West and Allen A. Knoll Publishers.

The bookstore offerings have grown tremendously in recent years. Borders joined another national chain store, Barnes & Noble, the independent Earthling Bookshop, and Chaucer & Co. as the largest stores in the area. Specialty books also are well represented. Sullivan Goss Books & Prints offers rare books and documents. The Book Den, the oldest bookstore in town, specializes in rare and unusual titles and may have the largest variety of books.

Publishers and bookstores thrive in large part because of Santa Barbara's lively literary community, which includes some famous writer residents. They include Sue Grafton, author of the best-selling Kinsey Millhone detective novels; T. Coraghessan Boyle, author of *The Road to Wellville*; Dennis Lynds (also known as Michael Collins),

The historic El Paseo restaurant, above, attracts visitors from all over the world. Right, ripe pinot noir grapes are readied for crushing at Sanford Winery in the Santa Ynez Valley. Valley vineyards produce some of the finest wines in the world.

author of the Dan Fortune mysteries; Marianne Williamson, author of *Illuminata*; and children's book authors Don and Audrey Wood (*King Bidgood's in the Bathtub* and *The Napping House*).

HIGH TECHNOLOGY

High-technology manufacturing suffered job losses in the early 1990s but is expected to stay relatively stable in coming years.

Applied Magnetics, the region's seventh-largest employer, makes magnetic recording heads for computer disk drives. The region's largest publicly traded company, it has struggled in recent years with declining revenues and layoffs. In late 1995, however, company officials announced a stabilization of the company and predicted future profitability. This revelation from a leader in the high-tech manufacturing industry was good news for the South Coast. Long accustomed to booming success, high-tech and defense-related companies suffered with defense cutbacks. Defense contractors Delco,

E-Systems, and Santa Barbara Research Center have all undergone layoffs.

Regenerating jobs to match the losses is a daunting task. But futuristic thinkers say growth in software development and the possible development of a commercial spaceport at Vandenberg Air Force Base (VAFB) in northern Santa Barbara County may help offset the losses.

VAFB officials and commercial interests expect the 98,000-acre base to become a primary launching facility for private companies over the next two decades. The base also serves as one of the military's most important rocket and missile test facilities. NASA is expected to launch some of its experimental space vehicles from Vandenberg as well.

OIL DEVELOPMENT

In the early 1980s, vast reserves of crude oil were found in pockets underlying the Santa Barbara Channel, prompting several large oil companies to push for development. The channel had been the site of oil exploration and

COMMUNICATIONS SATELLITES
on East Camino Cielo reveal the
march of high technology. Right,
a helicopter awaits visitors at
Santa Cruz Island at sunset.
Helicopter flights are a popular
mode of transportation to Santa
Cruz and other islands in the
Channel Islands National Park.

development for some years, but this vast find caused a flurry of activity and proposals for new platforms in the channel.

Ever since a 1969 well blowout in the channel, residents have been wary of oil production, even as they benefited from the taxes and jobs the industry brought to the South Coast. The spill blackened beaches for miles and spurred the nation's first environmental movement. Since discovery of the oil fields in the early 1980s, two major oil and gas facilities have been built on the Gaviota coast north of Santa Barbara, and a number of new platforms have been built in federal waters offshore.

All development has been done under strict county guidelines intended to protect the environmental integrity of the ocean and coast, as well as onshore air quality. There are more than 40 active leases in the channel that are available for development through the turn of the century. Experts say that because of improved technology it's likely that more oil will be produced from fewer platforms. Although five to seven new platforms will be added by about 2010, as many as 10 old platforms will be removed.

WINE COUNTRY

One local industry whose future definitely looks rosy is wine making. Since the first wineries began experimenting with Santa Ynez Valley wines in the late 1960s and early 1970s, the region has grown into one of the finest for grape growing and wine production in the world.

There are more than 30 wineries in the valley, many of which welcome visitors for tastings. More than 150,000 people visit tasting rooms annually, spending an average of $6 million on wine. The industry employs more than 2,500 people and contributes an estimated $17 million a year to the county economy.

The valley's wineries are not only a delight for wine aficionados but a fun attraction for tourists from all over the world.

TOURISM

Tourism is one of the South Coast's stalwart industries. Travelers' dollars make tourism the number-one contributor to the economy within the City of Santa Barbara and a dominant industry in the rest of the region.

Retailers and restaurants, motels and hotels all benefit from tourism, and the City and County of Santa Barbara work closely with the Santa Barbara and Goleta Valley Chambers of Commerce and the Santa Barbara Conference and Visitors Bureau to promote the region's attributes.

Nearly 100 hotels, motels, and bed and breakfast inns offer more than 4,800 rooms throughout the South Coast. And for large groups, Fess Parker's Red Lion Resort and the Four Seasons Biltmore have ample convention facilities: 38,000 square feet of space at the Red Lion and 15,000 square feet at the Biltmore.

The beachside Miramar, in Montecito, also has convention and banquet rooms. The Miramar hosts the Santa Barbara Writers Conference each June, a quarter-century tradition that brings together writers from all over the country for a week of talks, panels, workshops, and critique.

Tourists come to Santa Barbara for the obvious reasons: surf, sun, and sand. But they also are attracted by the region's world-class restaurants, entertainment, shopping, and wine country tours. Though visitor spending dipped a bit because of the recession in the early 1990s, occupancy rates at South Coast motels and hotels have surged in recent years.

Santa Barbara will always be a wonderful escape for those seeking a little piece of paradise.

THE FESS PARKER WINERY
on Foxen Canyon Road is one of
the newest wineries in the Santa
Ynez Valley. Founded by Fess
Parker, of "Davy Crockett" fame,
the winery features memorabilia
from Parker's long movie career.

SANTA BARBARA ENTERPRISE

WORKING IN SANTA BARBARA OFFERS OPPORTUNITIES TO EXPAND AND GROW, TO EXPLORE AND DREAM, TO DEVELOP NEW WAYS OF UNDERSTANDING— WHILE ENJOYING BEAUTIFUL SURROUNDINGS AND AN IDEAL CLIMATE. BUSINESS HERE IS SERIOUS BUT LAID BACK. CONTINUE ON FOR A LOOK AT SOME OF THE CORPORATIONS, PRO- FESSIONAL GROUPS, AND COMMUNITY SERVICE ORGANIZATIONS THAT ARE DOING BUSINESS SANTA BARBARA STYLE.

SANTA BARBARA
CHAMBER OF COMMERCE

letter from Stan Roden, 1996 chairman of the board of the Santa Barbara Chamber of Commerce:

Recently, the 1995 and 1996 Chamber boards met in a joint session. The purpose of the meeting was to create an agenda for 1996 and to set long-range goals for 1997 and 1998. The result was unanimous. We agreed to foster high-paying jobs—retain, replace, and recruit them; in short, economic development.

What does economic development mean? Isn't it a very complicated subject? Given the diversity of history and interests, a myriad of laws, politics, and economic forces, what can our Chamber effectively accomplish? How can so many different groups, at last count 16 in the area, with a single purpose to support economic development, act effectively without getting in each other's way?

A few days ago I stopped by a newly opened business on the way home from work. There were at least six employees working when I was there. The business probably employs 10 people overall. I started a conver-sation with the new owner by introducing myself as affiliated with the Santa Barbara Chamber.

I asked, "What was your experience in opening the business?"

He answered, "I was actively looking to locate in three or four different cities. In each one, I called the local Chamber. After my call to your Chamber, [Executive Director] Steve Cushman promptly returned my call and sent me an impressive package of information. I then visited Santa Barbara, and the Chamber put me in touch with the city permitting authorities."

"What made you finally choose Santa Barbara?" was my next question.

Without hesitation, he said, "Santa Barbara sold itself," and he quickly added that "the responsiveness of the Chamber was impressive."

When I asked if the city created difficult hurdles, he hesitated. "I lived in a special European city one time; I understand what Santa Barbara is trying to accomplish."

Responsiveness, communication, clearly stated and perceived goals, and cooperation are certainly part of the equation. There are, of course, others.

Affordable housing; adequate infrastructure; reliable and long-term water supplies and other utilities; accessible, affordable, and convenient transportation in and out of Santa Barbara, by road, rail, and plane; a local public education system that produces future workers, managers, and entrepreneurs who can function in the business world (i.e., think clearly, read and write effectively, and understand and operate modern equipment); local governments that are helpful, encouraging, and open to retention and expansion of existing businesses; a community that offers cultural amenities; and, I am sure, many others.

Can our 1996-98 Chamber boards work to improve these important components of a healthy economic environment? We have, we are, and we will continue to do so in varied ways too numerous to mention in this limited space.

I have asked dozens of people to tell me in a word or two what is the single most important thing any Chamber can do to support economic retention and development. At a recent joint meeting of the Goleta and Santa Barbara Chambers' Issues/Government Relations

Committees, "attitude" was the answer from Jim Ludwig, Goleta Chamber president. "Imagine what the South Coast could accomplish if the car attendant at the Biltmore, the owner/CEO of one of Goleta's bigger industrial companies, the city or county permit person, and everyone in between acted in the belief that the South Coast was open to, supportive of, and interested in economic growth and vitality?"

Our Chamber thus makes a positive contribution with every phone call it returns to local or prospective businesses, every package of materials sent out, every question it answers in a timely and relevant manner, every meeting it supports between local business workers and owners having common interests, every meeting it attends with other groups and organizations dedicated to similar goals, and every positive dialogue with local government policy makers geared to enlist local government as a partner, not as an adversary, in economic health.

Your Chamber has the attitude. The South Coast is a great place to do business. At the same time and in the same breath, there is a lot we can do to make it better. Our work is cut out for us. It's worth the effort.

About the Chamber

On February 25, 1871, several local merchants established a Chamber of Commerce in the town and county of Santa Barbara "to promote trade, commerce and business intercourse with other communities, and to promote, as far as we are able, in all honorable ways, the prosperity of our town, county and people."

One of its first projects was to promote Santa Barbara as a health resort. The successful program drew the rich and famous from all over the world, who enjoyed the restorative qualities of the area. Many chose to remain here, bringing with them a passion for a clean and open environment and the cultural advantages most often associated with far larger communities.

The infamous 1925 earthquake marked a major turning point in the history of this community. The measure of Santa Barbara's greatness was not in the fact that the city was restored but in the way the restoration was conducted.

Once the dust settled, the city, spurred on by the Community Arts Association, set up an Architectural Board of Review. Present-day Santa Barbara evolved from that disaster in a weave of Old Spanish traditions, modern community spirit, and progressive city building that created a refreshingly different combination than one finds in the typical small city. Its citizens have set out to make the community not only beautiful but distinctive—the ideal environment in which to live, work, and do business.

CITY OF SANTA BARBARA

The City of Santa Barbara is working hard to improve and diversify its economic base while maintaining a strong commitment to environmental values and protection of its unique quality of life.

Through a combination of public and public-private investment, the city, through its redevelopment agency, has been active since the early 1970s in a number of projects aimed at rehabilitating property, creating jobs, and stimulating private business development and investment downtown and along the waterfront.

As you explore Santa Barbara, you will see evidence of the agency's contributions everywhere. Its premier project is Paseo Nuevo, a retail revitalization project developed through a public-private partnership in the 1980s. This award-winning shopping center consists of 400,000 square feet of retail space anchored by two department stores connected by colorful, landscaped paseos, or promenades. Also included in the center are specialty shops, an assortment of cafes and restaurants, and ample space for parking.

Three exciting projects designed to cultivate economic development are under way. The first of these projects, being developed through a public-private partnership with former actor Fess Parker, will enhance the city's waterfront. The agency is building a 10-acre public park; the Parker family will be developing a 150-room luxury hotel on the adjacent site.

The second project is the restoration of Santa Barbara's historic railroad station. The number of trains serving Santa Barbara continues to increase, and

visitors will soon be greeted by a beautifully renovated depot, a small public park, new lighting, and a convenient parking area. These two projects are expected to be completed by summer 1997.

In 1997, the agency will assist in building an extension of Garden Street to provide new access to the waterfront. This new street will facilitate the creation of a major educational/cultural center at the entrance to the city that will include a world-class aquarium, two major museums, a marketplace, and a family hotel and restaurant.

In 1994, the city adopted an economic development plan "to affect and stimulate the Santa Barbara economy through proactive collaboration, teamwork, and the establishment of partnerships with the business community, school districts, university and colleges, resulting in replacement of lost jobs, expansion of the diversity of the economic base, and an increase of economic activity for sustaining our local economy."

The city involved a number of local and regional economic development groups, including the Santa Barbara Chamber of Commerce, the Santa Barbara Industrial Association, the Santa Barbara Regional Economy Community Project, the Santa Barbara County Economic Development Commission, and the Mayor's Business Advisory Committee.

In addition, the city has established a home page on the Internet (http://silcom.com/s.bar) that contains a substantial amount of economic data and is linked to Santa Barbara companies that have also placed information on the Internet.

Santa Barbara also is at the forefront in exploring innovative transportation technology. An electric bus, created and produced here, is receiving international attention and is used by the Santa Barbara Metropolitan Transit District (MTD) on several routes. With assistance from the city, MTD has also implemented a highly successful electric shuttle service in the prime tourist areas of the waterfront and shopping areas downtown.

Designated as a "City of Vision" by the International Conference on Livable Cities, Santa Barbara carefully strives to achieve that delicate balance between economic vitality and preservation of its reputation as a "Refuge from the Commonplace."

SANTA BARBARA BANK & TRUST

Santa Barbara Bank & Trust (SBB&T) is the largest and strongest independent bank in Santa Barbara and Ventura Counties. Its customers receive the benefits of financial strength, breadth of services, a uniquely personal approach to customer service, and the region's largest locally headquartered trust and investment services division.

Santa Barbara Bank & Trust is proud to be recognized as one of the nation's best-managed banks and is consistently ranked as the area's highest-rated financial institution by nationally respected rating services.

At SBB&T, you'll find all the personal and business services you'll ever need. The bank offers a wide array of products and services, from checking to cash management, bank cards and business services to commercial loans, savings plans to investment management, and IRAs to employee benefit planning, plus other trademarked services you won't find elsewhere.

SANTA BARBARA BANK & TRUST
VISION

To be the financial services provider of choice in the communities and markets we serve through exceptional employees delivering legendary customer service.

SANTA BARBARA BANK & TRUST
CORE VALUES

- FOSTER EMPLOYEE COMMITMENT
- EXCEED CUSTOMER EXPECTATIONS
- SUPPORT OUR COMMUNITIES
- MAXIMIZE SHAREHOLDER RETURN

The bank's staff of responsive professionals have the expertise and authority to make decisions. They share a steadfast commitment to delivering highly personal attention and building genuine and enduring relationships.

As a community bank, Santa Barbara Bank & Trust knows it's important to contribute to the communities it serves. You will find staff working side by side with local residents at business, civic, charitable, and arts organizations throughout the area.

These are just a few of the reasons the readers of the *Santa Barbara News-Press*, *Business Digest*, and the *Santa Barbara Independent* rated Santa Barbara Bank & Trust best bank overall—and why Santa Barbara Bank & Trust serves more businesses in southern Santa Barbara County than the next four banks combined.

Santa Barbara Bank & Trust. It can help in ways you never knew existed.

EAGLE INN

The Eagle Inn, nestled just a block from the beach in Santa Barbara, has the old-world charm of a bed and breakfast with the convenience and comfort of a modern hotel.

The inn is a cozy getaway for travelers looking for a place for a brief stay, as well as for visitors planning to spend a longer time in sunny Santa Barbara.

In 1981, owners Alan and Janet Bullock converted an apartment building into this wonderful inn, which has been lovingly restored. The rooms are beautifully appointed in bright florals and vary in style to reflect different periods. Some feature four-poster beds, and each has a microwave oven and refrigerator. Several of the rooms have full kitchens, making a week- or month-long visit a relaxing and affordable option.

Alan and Janet discovered Santa Barbara in 1980 while vacationing away from duties at a hotel they owned in England. They were driving up the coast from Los Angeles to San Francisco and stopped in Santa Barbara for lunch. Lunch turned into dinner, and the stay extended to several days. They never made it to San Francisco and went home to England determined to come back to this part of the California coast to live.

The next year they found a historic apartment building on Natoma Avenue, just a block from Cabrillo Boulevard and practically within shouting distance of the harbor and marina. A number of fine restaurants are within walking distance. Stearns Wharf, at the foot of the city's main thoroughfare and just a few blocks away, offers restaurants, souvenir shops, boat tours, and many other amenities of interest to visitors.

A quick jaunt from the foot of the wharf up State Street, perhaps in one of the city's electric buses or an open-air trolley, takes one to the heart of the shopping district, where fine shops and cultural events offer unlimited attractions.

The Eagle Inn is distinctive for its Spanish colonial architecture.

At the end of the day, one can stroll along the beach as the sun slowly sinks into the ocean, or simply relax at the Eagle Inn before venturing out for a fine dinner on the town. Later, one can settle down in the comfort of a cozy room to await the sunrise and the promise of a new day.

The building that now houses the Eagle Inn was constructed in the late 1920s by C. Cicero and is distinctive not only for its Spanish colonial architecture but for the cast-stone ornamentation of a large eagle on the front of the building. The Bullocks named the inn after this interesting detail. Cast-stone ornamentation was common in other parts of California during the Spanish colonial revival period but is unusual in Santa Barbara. The inn also features pointed arched doorways in the Moorish style, also rare in Santa Barbara.

The Eagle Inn offers a variety of rooms with queen-size and twin beds, with or without kitchens. A continental breakfast is included in the inn's reasonable rates. A bridal suite features a Southwest-style fireplace and private patio.

The Eagle Inn provides both intimacy and charm — a wonderful combination that is sure to make a visit

Full kitchens are a popular amenity at the Eagle Inn.

to Santa Barbara delightful and unique. The Eagle Inn welcomes you to Santa Barbara, our "Paradise on the Pacific."

Staying at the Eagle Inn is almost as comfortable as being at home.

CASA DORINDA

asa Dorinda, nestled between the foothills of the Santa Ynez Mountains and the Pacific Ocean, offers estate living on the California Riviera.

This beautiful retirement community is situated on 48 lush acres in Montecito. Originally the estate of Mr. and Mrs. William Bliss, Casa Dorinda opened as a retirement community in 1975. Today, it is home to just under 300 people. The original Mediterranean-style mansion is the center of many activities for residents and offers a rich and varied library, a game room, and reception rooms for social gatherings.

Casa Dorinda has everything—security, serenity, style, and gracious living. A professional staff provides unequaled service in food, maintenance, housing care, transportation, and lifetime health care. A full-time activity director arranges quality shows and cultural events, including trips to Los Angeles. Apartments are available in various sizes, from cozy studios to homes with two or more bedrooms and 1,600 square feet.

An on-site medical staff ensures that every need is met. Should a resident require more extensive atten-tion, Casa Dorinda guarantees lifetime care in state-of-the-art medical facilities. A brand-new medical center offers 52 private-only rooms.

The estate features extensive gardens and walking paths that wind through acres of sycamore and oak groves. Lawn bowling, croquet, swimming in the community pool, or relaxing in the jacuzzi are just a few of the activities available to Casa Dorinda residents. Nearby, they can enjoy golf, beaches, bikeways, tennis, sailing, fishing, first-class restaurants, and elegant shops. Cultural and arts offerings include the University of California at Santa Barbara, the Santa Barbara Museum of Art, the Music Academy of the West, the Natural History Museum, the Santa Barbara Zoo, the Santa Barbara Historical Society, and high-quality productions by several theater companies.

These recreational options combined with the exquis-ite care provided at Casa Dorinda make life here carefree. It is truly the finest in estate retirement living.

Casa Dorinda, located at 300 Hot Springs Road in Montecito, is accredited by the Continuing Care Accreditation Commission and is owned and operated by the not-for-profit Montecito Retirement Association.

FRANK SCHIPPER
CONSTRUCTION COMPANY

"Quality without Compromise" is more than a motto for Frank Schipper Construction Company of Santa Barbara. It's a way of life.

Owner Frank Schipper ensures that this commitment is evident in every decision and effort in which the company is involved, from reconstructing the public-access stairway leading to Miramar Beach in Montecito to renovating in record time Wells Fargo Bank in downtown Santa Barbara. Both projects won prestigious Associated General Contractors of California awards for the company.

Schipper, who founded his company in 1982 after 17 years with another major contractor, believes first in providing quality work at the very best value for the dollar. The way he goes about it is through teamwork. Schipper credits his chief estimator, John R. Hyde, Jr., and his general manager, Paul Wieckowski, with helping to ensure that teamwork is a company hallmark. The firm is proud of its reputation for working with clients and designers to bring about timely and cost-effective high-quality results. Schipper's son, Arlan, recently joined the company as a project engineer and estimator.

Schipper Construction specializes in commercial/industrial construction, seismic renovations, tenant improvements, and design-build projects. In 1993, Frank Schipper Construction Company won the Santa Barbara Contractors Association Builders Award for New Commercial/Industrial Construction and Commercial/Industrial Remodel. In 1994, Schipper Construction again won the Builders Award for Commercial/Industrial Remodel.

In addition to Wells Fargo and the beach access, recent multimillion-dollar projects Schipper is proud to have produced include a 34,000-square-foot renovation of El Montecito Presbyterian Church, construction of the 16,000-square-foot Carpinteria Girls, Inc., facility, a seismic upgrade of the historic Lobero Theatre in Santa Barbara, and construction of the 14,000-square-foot Channel Islands surgicenter in Oxnard. In 1995, the company undertook construction of a $9.3 million skilled nursing facility at Casa Dorinda in Montecito.

Schipper, "Skip" to his friends, strongly believes in giving back to the community and in doing what he can to counter his industry's sometimes less-than-positive reputation.

Schipper is active in the Santa Barbara Contractors Association and serves as chairman of the statewide Associated General Contractors of California (AGCC) Open Shop Committee. He also serves on the AGCC Building Division Board and the State Board. As chairman of the Open Shop Committee, Schipper was responsible for creating state-approved apprenticeship training programs for workers throughout the state in the open-shop construction trades.

Wells Fargo Bank

Schipper also is an active member of the Santa Barbara Suburban Kiwanis, the Goleta Valley Bicycling Club, and the American Mensa Society.

The company also assists Schipper's wife, Ellen, who owns and operates the Ellen Schipper Classical Ballet School and the nonprofit West Coast Ballet. Every year the West Coast Ballet stages *The Nutcracker* for the community, and Schipper Construction is proud to support the effort with props and other contributions.

Over the years, integrity, flexibility, teamwork, and community spirit have made Frank Schipper Construction Company one of the region's most successful contractors.

SANTA BARBARA MUNICIPAL AIRPORT

Santa Barbara Municipal Airport is the community's gateway to the world. Nine commercial airlines serve more than half a million passengers every year. Airport services include seven rental car companies, a restaurant, a gift shop, four airfreight operators, and several other services that make air transportation from Santa Barbara both convenient and pleasant.

The airport, which is owned and operated by the City of Santa Barbara, is self-supporting, bringing in revenue through user fees and tenant rents. With its red-tile roof, stucco facade, and iron ornamentation typical of the Spanish colonial revival architectural style, the historic airline terminal is a beautiful tribute to Santa Barbara. When visitors alight from a flight, this gracious, welcoming structure evokes a romanticism reminiscent of the city itself.

But there's much more to the Santa Barbara Municipal Airport than image.

With more than 2,000 employees and a payroll of $39 million a year, the airport is one of the largest employers in Santa Barbara County. More than 100 aviation and commercial/industrial tenants contribute more than $76 million annually to the local economy. Another $9 million in taxes is paid locally by airport service providers and users.

A comprehensive plan has been developed that will shape the future of this important regional facility, which totals 950 acres, into the twenty-first century.

Proposed aviation projects include extending the main runway by 400 feet and adding safety overrun areas at each end of the runway. Also proposed is the expansion of the airline terminal building.

The master plan includes proposed development of the airport's commercial/industrial property. High-technology incubator businesses, as well as light industrial, recreational, and retail uses, are being considered for this property.

There are more than 100 daily flights into and out of Santa Barbara Municipal Airport, making it the primary transportation hub in the county. About two-thirds of the quarter-million visitors who enter the city through the airport arrive on commercial airlines: Alaska Commuter Airlines, America West Express, American Eagle, Continental Connection, Northwest Airlink, Skywest/Delta Connection, United Airlines, United Express, and USAir Express. These airlines provide service to eight nonstop destinations and 100 one-stop destinations, including 17 foreign countries.

Recently renovated long-term and short-term parking lots provide passengers with improved access and convenience at reasonable rates.

More than 180 private aircraft are housed at the airport, and more than 80,000 visitors arrive each year by private plane, chiefly for business purposes. As businesses grow and visitors discover the fruits of this beautiful city, Santa Barbara Municipal Airport looks forward to providing continued excellent service well into the future.

PEPPER TREE INN

Santa Barbara is a favorite destination resort for both leisure and corporate visitors. Uniquely situated within the city are four hotels that offer the best in service, amenities, and location.

The BEST WESTERN PEPPER TREE INN is a full-service mini-resort located on State Street—Santa Barbara's "Main Street"—and adjacent to La Cumbre Shopping Plaza. The inn is minutes from the beach, downtown Santa Barbara, the Goleta business district, and area attractions.

Set on five landscaped acres, the Pepper Tree Inn features two tiled pools and whirlpools in garden courtyards. A sauna, an exercise room, massage facilities, and a restaurant/lounge are also located on the grounds of the hotel.

One hundred and fifty guest rooms offer terraces opening up to the pool and garden courtyards. Guest rooms include refrigerators, coffee makers, air conditioning, and fresh fruit and cookies.

The Pepper Tree Inn also offers three distinctive meeting rooms for conferences of up to 100 people.

The BEST WESTERN ENCINA LODGE & SUITES offers a quiet midtown location close to downtown shopping, restaurants, Sansum Medical Clinic, and Cottage Hospital.

The Encina Lodge has 121 guest rooms, including unique accommodations ranging from one-bedroom pool suites to two-bedroom apartments, all with fully equipped kitchens. Its additional features include a pool, whirlpool, sauna, and restaurant/lounge. The lodge is perfect for long-term visitors to Santa Barbara, businesspeople relocating to the area, and "snow birds."

Located two blocks from Santa Barbara's beach and scenic wharf area are the TROPICANA INN & SUITES and the INN BY THE HARBOR. The inns are ideally located for families, people who are relocating, and snow birds who would like to be near the beach. Each inn features a heated pool and whirlpool.

The Tropicana Inn offers 31 charming rooms decorated in country French decor. In addition to comfortable rooms with king-size and double beds, the Tropicana Inn has one-bedroom suites with living rooms and fully equipped kitchens.

The Inn by the Harbor features 43 rooms surrounding a tropical garden. Also decorated in country French decor, the inn has rooms with king-size beds and two beds as well as family suites with kitchens.

Beautiful pools and tropical gardens are features of the Best Western Pepper Tree Inn.

Santa Barbara County's United Way has three qualities that make it unique among charities:

- All the money and services it provides go to Santa Barbara County residents.
- It has a very high level of volunteer participation.
- Volunteer contributors decide where the money and management assistance go.

As a result, the United Way helps support a "Network for Caring" that includes up to 80 different organizations working together to improve the lives of area residents.

You & I

Helping Santa Barbarans Help Themselves

The Santa Barbara County United Way, established in 1923, has grown into a premier organization dedicated to solving the root problems that cause many of the social ills the organization was originally established to address. Typically, a United Way-assisted service in Santa Barbara coordinates its efforts and activities with two other United Way-assisted services. United Way's emphasis in recent years has been on helping people with limited resources or other problems find ways to improve their lives and become self-sufficient. The benefit is more successful outcomes for the same amount of money.

Santa Barbara County's United Way typically raises more than $2 million annually through fundraising efforts in workplaces and throughout the community. More than 14,000 working individuals and corporations contribute, as do more than 3,000 retirees. The money is distributed each year according to contributor survey results and the analysis of almost 200 volunteers, thus ensuring that the money is directed toward concerns that are priorities in the local community. In addition, more than 3,000 volunteers donate 60,000 hours a year to United Way efforts.

Recently, United Way began programs intended to help agencies provide services through collaboration and with the assurance of continuity. United Way's Linkages program offers money and assistance for special programs, such as one focused on gangs, to agencies willing to work together. The Successful Outcomes! program provides a three-year grant to agencies working on long-term, outcome-based projects that fall within the United Way's top three priority areas for dollars. Approximately one out of four county residents benefits from a United Way service in a year.

These new programs augment ongoing services that include helping people in crisis, strengthening youth, reinforcing families, improving health, and fighting alcohol and drug abuse in our communities.

With Santa Barbarans' help, Santa Barbara County United Way is making a difference.

BROWNING FERRIS INDUSTRIES
OF CALIFORNIA, INC.

Browning Ferris Industries of California, Inc., (BFI) has been a Santa Barbara County citizen since 1972, when it landed its first garbage collection and disposal contract with the City of Santa Barbara. Since then, BFI has grown along with the South Coast and now serves 25,000 residential customers and 3,400 commercial accounts throughout the region.

BFI offers its customers curbside recycling collection, backyard service for residences twice a week, commercial business collection services, "roll-off" debris boxes during temporary construction, and portable toilets. Over the years, BFI's attention to customer service, dependability, professionalism, and concern for the environment has earned the company respect from its customers and the community in general.

Out of special public-private partnerships has come a quick and sure helping hand when the community needed it. BFI provided free cleanup of debris after two devastating floods in early 1995. When a New Year's windstorm toppled untold numbers of trees in Santa Barbara in 1996, BFI was there again to haul away the debris at no cost to residents. When the county sheriff needed someone to transport a huge cache of seized marijuana, BFI was there to provide the service

free of charge. These are just a few examples of BFI's commitment to the community.

Equally impressive are the company's efforts to promote recycling. The company has become a leading collector of recyclables on the South Coast and introduced its "Mobius" recycling curriculum in local schools via the "Looking Good Santa Barbara" campaign.

BFI contributes to the community's economic development efforts and its various service organizations as well. The company is a member of numerous economic development groups and is a sponsor of the Economic Forecast Project at the University of California at Santa Barbara. BFI employees donate their time to several organizations, including the Santa Barbara County Boys' and Girls' Club, the Visiting Nurse Association, Las Positas Park, the Santa Barbara Chamber of Commerce, United Way, the Boy Scouts of America, and many others. The company also contributes financially to many of these groups.

BFI's success is built on its collaboration with the Santa Barbara community and the respect it has earned from its customers. It looks forward to many more years as both a corporate citizen and an active member of the community.

BERMANT DEVELOPMENT COMPANY

Bermant Development Company (BDC), a privately held firm that develops and manages real estate properties and investments, is proud to contribute to the economic development and vitality of Santa Barbara County.

BDC helps build the infrastructure for companies that do business here. It caters to their needs. With its core commitment to integrity, quality, and follow-through, BDC has created and manages many successful projects in the county, especially office and research and development business parks.

Since its founding in 1983, BDC has been involved in the development, investment, and management of more than 1.3 million square feet of office, research and development, industrial, and retail space in Southern California valued in excess of $130 million. BDC manages more than 500,000 square feet of private business property in the Goleta area alone.

Santa Barbara Corporate Center

Led by President Jeffrey C. Bermant, the company strives to blend its knowledge of community needs with those of its clients, the institutional investors. Bermant understands the complexities of today's development world and is committed to excellence in every dimension, from planning to the construction of challenging build-to-suit structures to long-term management.

Teamwork is a key factor in BDC's success. The company works closely with clients and tenants. It offers several specific in-house services, including initial marketing studies and analysis, land-use evaluations, entitlement approvals from local governments, access to capital markets, project financial structuring, financial analysis and reporting, management of land planning and architectural design, construction management, marketing and leasing, and asset management.

In recent years, BDC has developed some of the most exciting business projects in Santa Barbara County. The new General Research Corporation building offers 80,000 square feet of office space. The award-winning University Business Center on Hollister Avenue is a 270,000-square-foot, master-planned research and development complex consisting of five buildings. Santa Barbara Tech Center, located near the university and the airport, offers 84,000 square feet of office and research and development space designed specifically to meet the needs of the local high-tech community. Also on Hollister Avenue, the 88,000-square-foot Santa Barbara Corporate Center offers special amenities designed to enhance the corporate image, including a two-story glass lobby, outdoor eating areas, basketball and volleyball courts, and commissioned artwork.

Bermant Development Company is committed to providing first-class service, characterized by its quality, honesty, and integrity, and to contributing to the community. It believes that by focusing on the needs of tenants, it can create environments that enable them to achieve maximum productivity, thereby creating the best long-term value for investors.

MARBORG INDUSTRIES

amily-owned, community-focused MarBorg Industries has provided Santa Barbarans with impeccable refuse collection and other waste management services for three generations. As times have changed and needs have dictated, MarBorg has become a leader in community-wide recycling efforts.

MarBorg has its roots in the founding of Channel Disposal in 1936 by Mario F. Borgatello and his brother. In 1955, Laura and Augusta began working with their brothers. In 1974, the family business was divided and Mario F. founded MarBorg with his sons, David and Mario A. At that time, Laura and Augusta also joined MarBorg. In 1979, Augusta retired. After 22 years, Laura is still working full time. In 1986, the third generation began careers at MarBorg, beginning with Theresa and continuing with Brian, Kathleen, Mario A. II, and Kerri. Today, these members of the family are leaders in this growing and progressive company with their fathers and grandfather. In 1995, MarBorg purchased Channel Disposal.

MarBorg is proud of its involvement in and commitment to Santa Barbara. The company contributes in many ways, offering a free annual cleanup week, free collection during local disasters, and support during community functions such as Earth Day. MarBorg also participates in numerous civic organizations, including Rotary International, Soroptimist International, and the three local Chambers of Commerce. As a result, residents have come to regard MarBorg as a trusted friend and neighbor who has the community's best interests in mind.

Waste management has changed over the years. When MarBorg first started in business, residents looked to the company primarily for the removal and handling of food waste. Today, MarBorg is a leader in recycling efforts and a major contributor to Santa Barbara's integrated waste management system. With state regulations requiring a 50 percent reduction in the waste entering the landfill by 2000, MarBorg has taken an aggressive approach to recycling. In step with the many changes MarBorg has made in recent years, MarBorg changed its name in 1996 as well. For 21 years the company was known as MarBorg Disposal Company. Today, this well-diversified company is MarBorg Industries.

Like other waste disposal companies, MarBorg is an active participant in a successful curbside recycling program. But MarBorg has gone a step further, focusing on salvaging lumber, concrete, metal, plasterboard, and other construction debris that typically ends up cluttering a landfill. In fact, MarBorg is the leader in recycling commercial construction trash, diverting an estimated 30,000 tons of waste each year. Future plans include a "green waste" program for recycling grass clippings and other yard waste.

The "green waste" program is just another example of the Borgatello family's commitment to the community and its long-term needs. After all, Santa Barbara's lush and pristine environment will be home to future generations of Borgatellos, too.

From left to right: Andrea Borgatello, Anthony Borgatello, Theresa Borgatello Delgadillo, Brian Borgatello, Mario A. Borgatello, Ida Borgatello, Judy Borgatello, Mario F. Borgatello (retired), Peggy Borgatello, Laura Borgatello, Kristine Borgatello, Augusta B. Lord (retired), Louise Borgatello, David Borgatello, Kathy Koeper, and Kerri Borgatello

WESTPAC SHELTER CORPORATION

estpac is a real estate development and management firm that handles a diversified, privately held investment portfolio. Westpac has been in business for more than 20 years in Santa Barbara and has operations throughout California, Arizona, and Hawaii.

At present, the company employs more than 150 people. Its two principal officers are President and CEO Alex N. Pananides and Chief Financial Officer Dean N. Pananides.

Alex Pananides has been active in the real estate investment field for over 30 years, during which time he has been involved with projects valued at over $350 million. He is a 1965 graduate of San Jose State University with a degree in business. Active in the community, Mr. Pananides has served as chairman of the University of California-Santa Barbara Foundation, trustee of the California State University Foundation (systemwide), and member of the Board of Laguna Blanca School in Santa Barbara.

Dean Pananides holds a Ph.D. from the University of California at Santa Barbara and studied law at Berkeley's Boalt Hall. He has been associated with Westpac for over 15 years.

In association with banks and private investors, Westpac and its principals have put together projects that include more than 2,000 apartment units, seven hotels, numerous condominiums and office buildings, and similar properties. As the company enters its third decade, it will continue to maintain its philosophy of developing exceptional investment opportunities, with a long-term objective of safeguarding capital while optimizing yields.

Dean Pananides (left) and Alex Pananides

INVESTEC

Investec is a full-service real estate investment company whose top priority is serving its clients' needs and interests while seeking profitable investment opportunities. Founded in 1983 by Kenneth Slaught, Investec offers consolidated services, from investment to construction and development to property management and sales and marketing. Over the years, Investec has established a reputation for trust and long-term reliability with real estate investors and owners. Acquisitions through 1996 were valued at more than $250,000,000.

Investec has continued to grow and increase its services. It is active in new construction and development, as well as the rehabilitation of existing properties. It is one of the premier home builders in Santa Barbara County and is the leading full-service real estate firm in Santa Barbara. Some of its more notable projects include Arlington Court, a 17,000-square-foot office and residential development in downtown Santa Barbara, and the 255-unit El Escorial condominium project at East Beach. Investec specializes in environmental sensitivity and in building consensus between landowners, environmentalists, and local government.

In 1986, the **Investec Management Corporation** was created to handle associated property and asset management functions, and today it is a leader in its field. Investec Management Corporation provides comprehensive services in commercial and multifamily residential property asset management.

Investec's **Sales and Marketing Division** utilizes diverse and unique skills to achieve maximum price and absorption rate. Flexibility and breadth of services create a competitive advantage unmatched in the field.

INVESTEC CONSTRUCTION, INC., is a full-service construction company that handles all aspects of the firm's building needs. Cost-conscious building and pooling of resources enable Investec to build at significantly lower costs than other firms.

Future success in the real estate investment field depends on the disciplined management of capital and the consolidated availability of services. Only those firms with proven results and responsible acquisition criteria will thrive in today's business climate. Investec will be among them.

Investec provides a complimentary newsletter for all clients detailing progress on existing projects and offering notices of upcoming investment opportunities. For a copy, call (805) 962-8989.

Arlington Court in downtown Santa Barbara

TRABUCCO & ASSOCIATES/TRABUCCO COMMERCIAL CONSTRUCTION

T RABUCCO & ASSOCIATES and TRA-BUCCO COMMERCIAL CON-STRUCTION, INC., have been responsible for the development of high-quality residential and commercial construction projects throughout the tricounty area and beyond. Owner Andy Trabucco states that the two companies are guided by an overriding philosophy: "Every building endeavor consists of three key elements—time, cost, and quality. Our companies' goal is to maximize these elements to create the best product possible given the project's particular constraints."

TRABUCCO & ASSOCIATES and TRA-BUCCO COMMERCIAL CONSTRUCTION, INC., specialize in fast-tracked projects and pride themselves on the quick completion of top-quality construction, from housing to major commercial developments.

The firms' president, Andy Trabucco, his wife, Robin, and their two children have lived in Santa Barbara for more than 15 years. Andy Trabucco has been in the construction business since 1976 and founded his own construction company in 1981. Robin Trabucco, who has been involved in corporate accounting and office management since 1977, oversees the accounting operations for the two companies.

TRABUCCO & ASSOCIATES started out specializing in residential projects and custom homes and took on commercial projects only occasionally. Then, in 1989, market changes opened up the opportunity to expand the firm's foothold in the commercial arena. This resulted in the creation of TRABUCCO COMMERCIAL CONSTRUCTION, INC.

The focus on commercial construction and development in recent years has allowed for a strong partnership with Bermant Development Company and the successful completion of many prominent commercial projects. Among the companies' large corporate clients are Mentor Corporation, PS Medical, Tenet Healthcare, and GRC International.

The entire team at TRABUCCO assists clients in making educated decisions throughout the development process, from initial design and budgeting to actual construction, while providing ongoing opportunities for creativity. In this vein, TRABUCCO & ASSOCIATES has built more than 240 homes, condominiums, and apartments in Santa Barbara County, and TRABUCCO COMMERCIAL CONSTRUCTION, INC., has already constructed well over 400,000 square feet of commercial projects.

Through an abundance of "word-of-mouth" referrals and an effective marketing program, as well as competent project management and fast-paced schedules, TRABUCCO & ASSOCIATES and TRABUCCO COMMERCIAL CONSTRUCTION, INC., are continually enlarging the circle of clientele for whom they are providing quality construction.

SOUTHERN CALIFORNIA EDISON

southern California Edison, a proud member of the Edison International family of companies, has a long tradition of excellent service. In the late 1880s, Edison's ancestral utilities—the first in Visalia and the second in Santa Barbara—supplied rudimentary electric service to a dozen customers. From these beginnings, far-sighted pioneers worked to produce a reliable supply of electricity to light the homes and streets, power the factories and businesses, and irrigate the fields and orchards of Southern and Central California.

While the early Visalia system got off to a shaky start, Santa Barbara Electric Light Company enjoyed great popular support in the community. Circuits 1 and 2 were switched on at 7 P.M. on March 15, 1887. For the first time, brilliant light shone from 15 tall masts along State Street and the 150-foot iron tower at State and Victoria Streets, as well as the post office, the San Marcos Hotel, and several residences and nearby buildings.

From these early beginnings, Southern California Edison has grown to be one of the nation's largest utilities, serving 4.2 million people in a 50,000-square-mile service territory. With more than a century of experience, Edison strives to provide customers with innovative energy-related products, services, and information, while lowering prices.

The company has pledged to lower prices by 25 percent (adjusted for inflation) by the year 2000.

Southern California Edison has also created a robust portfolio of innovative energy solutions for business customers, helping them achieve growth and profitability.

FLEXIBLE PRICING OPTIONS

- Economic development prices to encourage business startup, retention, and expansion
- Special pricing programs for agricultural customers
- Environmental pricing programs for customers who install electric technologies with proven environmental benefits

ENERGY SOLUTIONS

- Consulting and technical and design services for energy management, central cooling, and new construction
- Energy audits for large customers and self-audits for small commercial and industrial customers
- Power quality analysis
- CTAC and AgTAC, Edison's electric solutions centers, provide technology and product demonstrations and seminars.

ENVIRONMENTAL APPLICATIONS

Southern California Edison's environmental consulting services help customers comply with stringent air- and water-quality standards with cost-effective, environment-friendly electric technologies that can help businesses.

BILLING OPTIONS

Summary Billing consolidates all of a customer's statements into one bill.

Diskette Billing delivers customers' Edison bills as electronic data, helping them to manage budgets and energy.

Electronic Data Interchange allows customers to receive and pay their bills electronically.

COX COMMUNICATIONS

A fter 24 years, Cox Communications has become an integral part of the Santa Barbara landscape. Among the nation's top five cable television operators, Cox Communications has invested heavily in both state-of-the-art technology and customer service.

In Santa Barbara alone, Cox has invested more than $32 million in infrastructure upgrades in the last five years, including replacing 118 miles of cable with fiber-optics by the end of 1996, purchasing a permanent facility, and constructing a signal reception facility.

"We continue to upgrade our system to support a vast array of upcoming voice, video, and data services," says Jill Campbell, general manager. "We're also investing heavily in customer service, the foundation of the business, to ensure we're prepared to provide innovative new services to our customers." Cox Communications Santa Barbara has been awarded the prestigious National Cable Television Association's "Seal of Good Customer Service" for five consecutive years.

Besides providing 78 channels through its local fiber-optic cable service, Cox Communications Santa Barbara offers its customers the Primestar satellite service, Music Choice digitized radio, and Ingenious X-Change, an educational computer information service. Cox Communications, since its recent merger with the Times Mirror systems, has also become a partner in a joint venture with Sprint and two other cable companies to offer competitive wired and wireless local and long-distance telephone services in the near future.

Cox Communications Santa Barbara also contributes significantly to the community it serves by providing financial and in-kind donations to charitable organizations and enabling employees to do volunteer service. Among some of the ways in which Cox contributes to local activities are the following:

- providing free admission to several local museums
- donating over $12,000 annually to the United Way
- offering local nonprofit organizations production services and air time

- contributing $5,000 in educational scholarships through the Santa Barbara Scholarship Foundation.

Cox Communications embraces its partnership with the educational community. Support includes free cable service to all local schools, as well as special events and services, including "Movie Critic for the Day," "Scouting for Food," and video equipment grants. Cox Communications Santa Barbara has been recognized for its continued commitment to education with the "Golden Apple" award from the Santa Barbara County Schools and the "Beacon Award" for educator outreach.

Cox Communications Santa Barbara also provides the Santa Barbara community with a newly renovated public access studio, funded and managed as a special service to community members interested in learning all aspects of television production.

KCOX, Cox's community events station, educates and informs the South Coast community by providing local coverage of political and business events, interviews with local state and federal officials, high school football games, parades, and other civic activities.

Last year, Cox Communications' total economic impact on the communities it serves reached $41 million, including franchise fees, taxes, salaries, and benefits.

"Cox Communications is part of the local community, not only through providing cable services but through each employee," says Jill Campbell. "Our company's future is intertwined with the future of the South Coast community."

SANSUM MEDICAL CLINIC

ansum Medical Clinic has a strong reputation locally and nationally for providing state-of-the-art medical services and personalized care in a warm and friendly environment. Since its founding in 1924, Sansum has achieved acclaim as a leading health-care provider for medical evaluation, diagnosis, and treatment.

Comprising a team of over 70 board-certified specialists representing 35 distinct areas of health care, Sansum Medical Clinic emphasizes the importance of individualized health care.

Sansum Medical Clinic has a long and proud heritage. In 1920, Dr. William David Sansum came to Santa Barbara as the director of the Potter Metabolic Clinic, where he specialized in the research and treatment of diabetes. Dr. Sansum dedicated himself to discovering cures for the disease and is credited with being the first American to successfully isolate, produce, and administer insulin to treat diabetes.

To meet the changing needs of the Santa Barbara community, especially in the areas of managed care and health maintenance organizations (HMOs), Sansum Medical Clinic has initiated a complementary network of primary care centers throughout the area. These centers are used by HMO patients and are supported by the specialists at the Clinic.

Meeting the growing needs of employers is a high priority within the Sansum network of health-care centers. Sansum provides an Executive Health Program and VIP Program to keep personnel healthy through periodic physical examinations. Corporations send their employees to Sansum from all over the country to participate in this detailed and comprehensive health-screening program.

Sansum Medical Clinic's services are available through physician referral or self-referral. To make an appointment, call (805) 682-2621 or, from outside Santa Barbara County, toll-free (800) 4-SANSUM.

ST. FRANCIS MEDICAL CENTER

St. Francis Medical Center is a nonprofit community hospital operated by the Franciscan Sisters of the Sacred Heart. Nearly 450 physicians practice more than 25 specialties at this full-service hospital.

St. Francis has been providing high-quality health care to the Santa Barbara community for nearly 100 years, serving people from all walks of life and of all faiths. The hospital's state-of-the-art medical facilities and services include the cozy and intimate Family Birth Center, Magnetic Resonance Imaging (MRI), a CT scanner, the Cardiac Catheterization Laboratory, an expanded Emergency Center, Surgical Suites, the Transitional Care Unit, outpatient care services, and a senior assisted-living residence, known as Villa Riviera.

Founded in 1908 by the Franciscan Sisters of the Sacred Heart, St. Francis has grown from a tiny sanitorium the Sisters purchased from a trio of physicians. When the 1925 earthquake destroyed the structure, the Sisters resolved to rebuild, and were joined in the effort by the community.

Since then, St. Francis has been through numerous major expansions, including the addition of a new surgical wing in 1986 and completion of the Family Birth Center in 1987. Since 1991, the hospital has added MRI and the Cardiac Catheterization Laboratory, the Transitional Care Unit, and Villa Riviera. In 1995, St. Francis launched its Congregational Healthcare (Parish Nursing) Program, designed to reach out and provide health care to the community in conjunction with local congregations.

Today, St. Francis is a vibrant medical center with a reputation for tender nursing care and keen attention to patient needs. The hospital has maintained a competitive position in today's dynamic health-care marketplace and is poised to serve the community well into the twenty-first century.

In this way, St. Francis continues its mission to provide its neighbors with the highest-quality health care possible.

HORIZON PRODUCTIONS

Santa Barbara once was home to one of the largest movie studios in the world, rivaling Hollywood. With advances in communications, Hollywood is coming back to Santa Barbara. Producers of film and video projects can complete their projects with all the technological advances available to them in Los Angeles—but in a stunning, less stressful setting that allows creative energies to unfold. Founded in 1992, Horizon Productions in downtown Santa Barbara brought nonlinear editing technology to a growing production community.

An award-winning Horizon Productions team delivers cutting-edge film and video projects—from concept to final cut—in Santa Barbara's first fully on-line, all-AVID production studio. Whether the client is a seasoned pro or a first-time producer, the editors, producers, and videographers at Horizon work hard to make the job easy. Horizon does it with the help of sophisticated AVID Media Composer technology.

AVID is the industry's most powerful on-line, digital, nonlinear editing system. It provides virtually unlimited freedom to create. There's no waiting for tape, no linear limitations. Just pure creativity.

For Web home pages, interactive displays, electronic catalogs, the latest in LCD projector technology for presentations, and complete CD-ROM production, step into Horizon's Multimedia Suite. With a 132-MHz PowerMac PCI 9500 running the industry's most powerful authoring software (Authorware and Director) and updated 3D modeling and animation from Macromedia and Strata, clients are catapulted into the expanding world of Internet and interactive multimedia communications. Horizon's designers and technicians keep clients in touch with the latest trends in this exciting new domain.

Horizon Productions is the answer when time is short or production staff too busy. Horizon's experienced team has produced results-oriented sales presentations, infomercials, commercials, and marketing videos for national and international markets. Horizon is a turn-key production solution when the job must be done right, on time and on budget, the first time.

Horizon Productions—Santa Barbara's communications company on the edge.

CAL WEST GROUP, INC.

The Cal West Group, Inc., is a management company that was formed in 1984 by Richard Berti to oversee his holdings in Santa Barbara: the Santa Barbara Athletic Club; the Cathedral Oaks Tennis, Swim and Athletic Club; and Lyon Moving and Storage, as well as various real estate properties.

Founded in 1978 as the Santa Barbara Racquetball Club, the Santa Barbara Athletic Club (SBAC) is the area's premier fitness club. Since its first years, the downtown Santa Barbara club has grown in membership and services. Today, it caters to Santa Barbara's elite, with state-of-the-art fitness equipment, racquetball and squash courts, aerobics and weight rooms, a child care center, and many other amenities. In 1992, *Shape* magazine selected the club as one of the top 10 lifestyle/wellness centers in the United States. Its full-service fitness center offerings are complemented by the luxuries of a country club, including courts, jacuzzis, saunas, steam rooms, a swimming pool, an outdoor exercise area for aerobics and weight training, and extensive social activities.

The club also acts as a primary business network for corporate patrons, who make up 40 percent of its membership. Many business deals are rumored to have been struck on the courts and in the locker rooms!

Recent research has shown that physical fitness can be preventive medicine. SBAC works closely with the medical community to help members achieve and retain top physical conditioning and health.

That same commitment can be found at Cathedral Oaks Club, where the focus is on family fitness, particularly through swimming and tennis. Cathedral Oaks Club, located at 5800 Cathedral Oaks Road in Goleta, was founded in 1975.

The club's "resort" feeling is complemented by the quiet location, lush landscaping, and spacious facility. There are 12 tennis courts (8 of which have night lighting), two heated pools, a state-of-the-art aerobics studio, fitness facilities, two locker rooms, saunas, jacuzzis, and a cafe and pro shop on the premises. The club also offers free nutritional counseling, fitness instruction, and fitness consultations.

Cathedral Oaks Club has an active and enthusiastic tennis membership and offers a wide variety of swim programs for children and adults. A special part of the club is its family-membership orientation. Cathedral

Oaks Club offers exceptional child care, as well as instruction for children in swimming, tennis, ballet, and karate. Teen classes are also available in the fitness department. Special family events, such as the annual Fourth of July barbecue, contribute to keeping families active together.

Lyon Moving and Storage has a rich and storied past in Santa Barbara. Located at 27 East Cota Street, Lyon celebrated its 110th anniversary in 1996. It's come a long way since those days of mules and dray wagons.

The company has its roots in one John Redmond Lathim, a Missourian who arrived in Santa Barbara in 1883. He went to work for the Wentling Trucking Company but soon opened his own firm, Lathim Express Company. Lathim did well, but it was his son, Ray, born just before the turn of the century, who, in exercising some entrepreneurial savvy, built the company into a major success.

In 1912, when Ray was just 19 years old, he sold all his mules and wagons and purchased a ton-and-a-half, two-cylinder auto car truck. It was the first in Santa Barbara. Lathim's business grew.

As time went on, Lathim built the warehouse that still stands on Cota Street and struck his first-ever labor contract. In 1928, he fostered a deal with the owners of seven other moving companies between Santa Barbara and San Francisco. Thus was born the Lyon Moving and Storage Company. It's new logo: "Let Lyon Guard Your Goods!"

The Lathim family sold its final interest in the company in 1980, but Lyon continues to carry on a long tradition. Today, Lyon is an Allied Van Lines agent whose logo still imparts the basis for its success: a trusted company that provides quality moving and storage services with pride, at reasonable costs.

As part of the Cal West Group, Inc., the two clubs and Lyon work closely together, contributing to the company's strength and bright future.

All the Cal West Group, Inc., businesses can be found on the Internet at the Web site address: http://www.calwestgroup.com.

QAD Inc.

One of the world's leading integrated business software companies, QAD Inc. is also one of the region's best citizens.

The employee-owned company supports numerous charitable and business organizations throughout the year in both Santa Barbara and Ventura Counties. Contributions have been made to various local organizations that promote community, education, the arts, and social welfare, including the Santa Barbara Hospice, the Santa Barbara Rape Crisis Center, Ojai Valley Community Church, the Lobero Theatre in Santa Barbara, the Carpinteria Unified School District, Buena High School in Ventura, Christmas Unity, and the California AIDS Ride. Donations have also been made to such national societies as Habitat for Humanity and the American Cancer Society. The company's Charities Committee coordinates donations and matches each employee's contribution to these and other charitable organizations.

Each spring QAD proudly participates in Ventura County's Corporate Challenge, a round-robin tournament featuring a wide range of businesses from the entire South Coast. Sporting events include volleyball, swimming, golf, billiards, softball, and a dozen others.

Participation in this annual event has served to generate company spirit, to gain the company visibility, and to encourage camaraderie among employees.

QAD is a proud "Gold Sponsor" of the Carpinteria Chamber of Commerce Awards and is an active member of such business groups as the South Coast Business and Technology Council in Santa Barbara and the Educational Society for Resource Management, a professional global organization focusing on manufacturing standards. In 1995, QAD earned the Company of the Year award from the South Coast Business and Technology Council.

Founded in 1979 by Pamela and Karl Lopker, QAD is a premier developer of computer software that assists manufacturers in producing and tracking their products. Clients include such multinational companies as Coca-Cola, Quaker Oats, AT&T, Johnson & Johnson, Black and Decker, 3M, Philips, Matsushita, Ford Motor Company, Daewoo, Glaxo, and Unilever.

QAD's flagship product, MFG/PRO®, is a software solution that provides a global supply chain management approach from initial design to end product, including manufacturing, distribution, and financial and customer service applications. The

software is designed to run on any UNIX or Windows NT computer system and enables manufacturers to manage multi-site inventories from off-site locations. QAD designs MFG/PRO to fit the needs of specific markets such as the automotive, electronics/industrial, food and beverage, consumer packaged goods, and medical industries and provides subsequent technical support. MFG/PRO is available in 24 languages and has been implemented in 70 countries.

MFG/PRO was initially developed by Pamela Meyer Lopker, President of QAD. A graduate of the University of California at Santa Barbara, Pamela created a forerunner of MFG/PRO for the Hewlett-Packard 250 prior to investing early in a UNIX-based MFG/PRO. One of her first customers was Deckers, a shoe manufacturer based in Carpinteria and founded by Karl Lopker. Karl left Deckers to help establish QAD and is now the company's CEO.

In the mid-1980s, the Lopkers redesigned MFG/PRO in an "open-system" framework, capable of running on various computer platforms. They also decided to market their software internationally. Both proved to be momentous decisions. QAD experienced phenomenal growth—in some years as much as 80 percent. Today, about 60 percent of QAD's sales derive from international relationships. The company has offices in 17 countries but maintains its headquarters on the South Coast, where its offices are located in Carpinteria and in Summerland overlooking the vast Pacific.

As part of its commitment to its customers, QAD sponsors an annual Worldwide User Conference called Explore, which draws more than 1,200 QAD customers and partners. This springtime event uses

Pamela Meyer Lopker, President

materials printed and designed by numerous graphics professionals from the Santa Barbara area. In addition, every January the company hosts its entire sales force locally for a week-long sales kickoff meeting intended to encourage another year of prosperous sales.

QAD has established QAD University, known as "QU," an ongoing program that educates employees, customers, and business partners on MFG/PRO and QAD's business practices and values. Sessions are held each month and attract people from all parts of the world. Since QAD maintains its headquarters locally, frequent corporate visits from prospective customers and partners also contribute tourist dollars to the local economy.

QAD's success is due in large part to its commitment to its employees. When QAD's growth made it clear that the company had to expand its headquarters, the Lopkers chose to purchase two South Coast sites—a 28-acre property on Ortega Hill in Summerland and a 33-acre parcel in Carpinteria—rather than move out of the area. The Lopkers believe their employees are the brain trust of their business and are worth the extra effort and cost to retain them.

As international growth and success escalate for the company, QAD continues to expand locally, committed to serving its employees and its community and striving through each endeavor to create Paradise on the Pacific.

RAYTHEON/E-SYSTEMS GOLETA DIVISION

In the quiet ambience of Santa Barbara, with its rich culture and panoramic beauty, is an organization known for its commitment to innovative technology, hard work, and community citizenship for over 40 years.

E-Systems (until 1995, known as Raytheon) Goleta Division began in 1956 when the Raytheon Manufacturing Company bought the 15-acre Williams Ranch. At the time, the community of Goleta was known primarily for its lemon and avocado orchards. But it was an attractive area for the company because of its ideal geographic proximity to three major customer groups: Vandenberg Air Force Base, the Navy's Point Mugu, and aircraft companies in the Los Angeles area.

A contemporary building was constructed on this ranch site, and five more buildings, an antenna testing range, and a reflecting pool were later added. This campus is now located about half a mile from the new division headquarters on Los Carneros Road. At this 67-acre site near the Santa Barbara Municipal Airport is a modern 100,000-square-foot office building and a 100,000-square-foot state-of-the-art manufacturing facility with a controlled temperature and humidity system, the latest automatic storage and retrieval system, and the newest manufacturing and testing capabilities.

In 1995, the Raytheon Company acquired Texas-based E-Systems and announced that its operation in Goleta would become a division of E-Systems. This change was made to take advantage of the synergistic business opportunities that were apparent between E-Systems and the Goleta Division.

In the early years, the division was a research and design facility that produced components for a variety of government programs. All that changed in the 1970s when the organization successfully bid on a multiyear program to design, develop, and manufacture the U.S. Navy's standard on-board electronic countermeasures protection systems for the surface fleet. Known as the AN/SLQ-32, this product helped transition this dynamic organization into a major manufacturing facility.

These and other innovative electronic principles were expanded in the 1980s and 1990s into aerial decoys, airborne high-power jamming, self-protect systems, and other programs in support of U.S. Department of Defense initiatives.

In addition to its core defense electronics business, E-Systems is researching new ways to apply its advanced digital signal processing technology to military, commercial, and global markets. The newest and most promising of these commercial programs is called Millennium. Funded in part by an award from the U.S. Advanced Research Projects Agency, Millennium involves the development of wideband digital telecommunications technology.

The Millennium receiver technology being developed by E-Systems is characterized by extraordinarily large bandwidths and dynamic range and improved processing speed and information capacity. This technology provides three times the instantaneous processing bandwidth, samples signals at six times current clock rates, and processes data at better than eight times the rate of currently available commercial technologies.

Difficult to grasp? Think of the fastest PC available today, then imagine how fast it will be in six years. That's the type of technology available today from the competent and diverse staff at E-Systems Goleta Division. Commercial application of this technology will involve a variety of products, such as local and wide-area switching networks, routers, on-board and ground-based satellite and cellular transceivers, military and commercial radars, integrated radio frequency avionics, and

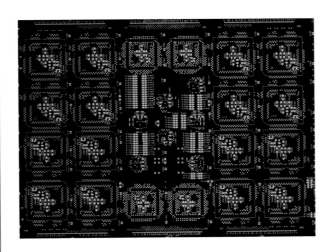

special receivers that will allow users to move into the passing lane of the Information Superhighway. In addition to sophisticated commercial applications, the technology will continue to be applied to the military marketplace, enabling quantum leaps in performance for communications, electronic warfare, signal intelligence receivers, and surveillance systems for all of the U.S. armed forces.

These new and exciting developments will augment E-Systems' traditional work in electronic defense technology and help ensure long-term viability for the company.

In addition to these technical contributions, the company and its employees are known as leaders in community service. Their positive, "can-do" spirit touches a variety of local programs and organizations. Active sponsorship of many United Way activities and local universities, a special partnership program with San Marcos High School, as well as close long-term relationships with the Santa Barbara and Goleta Chambers of Commerce and other local organizations such as the Santa Barbara Industry Education Council and the Santa Barbara Industrial Association are among the key priorities.

These examples reinforce the commitment to "help make a difference" . . . and add to the cultural enrichment and true beauty of the Santa Barbara community.

ACKNOWLEDGMENTS

Each of the following organizations, health-care institutions, and government entities made a valuable contribution to this project. Longstreet Press gratefully acknowledges their participation.

Bermant Development Company
Browning Ferris Industries of California, Inc.
Cal West Group, Inc.
Casa Dorinda
City of Santa Barbara
Cox Communications
Eagle Inn
Frank Schipper Construction Company
Horizon Productions
Investec
MarBorg Industries
Pepper Tree Inn
QAD Inc.
Raytheon/E-Systems Goleta Division
St. Francis Medical Center
Sansum Medical Clinic
Santa Barbara Bank & Trust
Santa Barbara Chamber of Commerce
Santa Barbara Municipal Airport
Southern California Edison
Trabucco & Associates/Trabucco Commercial Construction
United Way
Westpac Shelter Corporation

This book was published in cooperation with the Santa Barbara Chamber of Commerce and would not have been possible without the support of its members. Longstreet Press is especially grateful to the following individuals for their commitment and continued assistance:

Stephen Cushman
Jeanne Maciej

The following publications were excellent sources of information for the text:

Advances in Research: Scientific Inquiry at the University of California Santa Barbara. University of California at Santa Barbara Office of Research, 1993.

Berger, John Anton. The Franciscan Missions of California. New York: G. P. Putnam Sons, 1941.

"Big Valley." Santa Barbara magazine. Oct/Nov. 1985.

Caldwell, Jayne Craven. Carpinteria as It Was. Papillon Press, 1979.

California's Chumash Indians. A project of the Santa Barbara Museum of Natural History Education Center. Santa Barbara: John Daniel, 1986.

Chesnut, Merlyn. The Gaviota Land: A Glimpse into California History from a Bend on El Camino Real. Santa Barbara: Fithian Press, 1993.

Chiacos, Elias. Mountain Drive: Santa Barbara's Pioneer Bohemian Community. Santa Barbara: Shoreline Press, 1994.

Conard, Rebecca, and Christopher H. Nelson. Santa Barbara, El Pueblo Viejo: A Walking Guide to the Historic Districts of Santa Barbara. Santa Barbara: Capra Press, 1986.

Coombs, Gary B., ed. Those Were the Days: Landmarks of Old Goleta. Goleta, Calif.: Institute for American Research, 1986.

Fagan, Brian M. Cruising Guide to California's Channel Islands. Marina del Rey, Calif.: Western Marine Enterprises, 1983.

Farley, Marco. The Legacy of Pearl Chase. Edited by Vivian Obern. Santa Barbara: Santa Barbara Trust for Historic Preservation, 1988.

Gardner, Theodore Roosevelt II. Lotusland: A Photographic Odyssey. Santa Barbara: Allen A. Knoll, 1995.

Gilbar, Steven, and Dean Stewart, compiler. Tales of Santa Barbara, from Native Storytellers to Sue Grafton. Santa Barbara: John Daniel & Co., 1994.

Grant, Campbell. The Rock Paintings of the Chumash. San Luis Obispo, Calif.: EZ Nature Books, in cooperation with the Santa Barbara Museum of Natural History, 1993.

Hawley, Walter A. The Early Days of Santa Barbara, California, from the First Discoveries by Europeans to December, 1846. 3d ed. Santa Barbara: Santa Barbara Heritage, 1987.

Jackman, Jarrell C. Santa Barbara Historical Themes and Images. Norfolk/Virginia Beach: Donning Co., 1988.

Kennedy, Roger G. Mission. New York: Houghton Mifflin, 1993.

Lambert, May. Growing Up with Summerland. Carpinteria, Calif.: Carpinteria Valley Historical Society, 1975.

Myrick, David F. Montecito and Santa Barbara. Vols. 1 and 2, From Farms to Estates. Glendale, Calif.: Trans-Anglo Books, 1987.

Nabokov, Peter, and Robert Easton. Native American Architecture. New York: Oxford University Press, 1989.

The Native Americans: An Illustrated History. Atlanta: Turner Publishing, 1993.

"Pride of the Valley." Santa Barbara magazine. Nov./Dec. 1983.

Santa Barbara County. Los Angeles: Automobile Club of California, 1988.

Staats, H. Philip, ed. Californian Architecture in Santa Barbara. Stamford, Conn.: Architectural Book Publishing, 1990.

Storke, Thomas M. California Editor. Los Angeles: Westernlore Press, 1958.

Tompkins, Walker A. It Happened in Old Santa Barbara. Santa Barbara: Santa Barbara National Bank, 1976.

Santa Barbara: Past and Present. Santa Barbara: Tecolote Books, 1975.

"Under Glass." Santa Barbara magazine. April/May 1986.

In addition, numerous articles in the Independent and in the Santa Barbara News-Press were extremely useful.

INDEX

INDEX FOR
ENTERPRISE SECTION